THE DARKLANDS

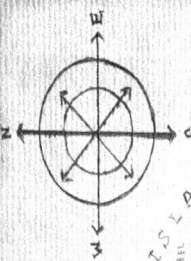

THE DARKLANDS

A MELANESIAN EXPERIENCE

BRANDON OSWALD

Publish Authority

The Darklands: A Melanesian Experience
Copyright © 2022 Brandon Oswald

ISBN 978-1-954000-31-5 (Paperback)
ISBN 978-1-954000-32-2 (eBook)

All events, locales, conversations, and observations in this book are from the author's memories of them and from his perspective.

Cover design lead: Raeghan Rebstock
Editors: Bob Laning and Nancy Laning

Published 2022, by Publish Authority
300 Colonial Center Parkway, Suite 100
Roswell, GA 30076-4892 USA
PublishAuthority.com

Printed in the United States of America

CONTENTS

For All Who Are Living the Melanesian Way

That the past is ahead, in front of us, is a conception of time that helps us retain our memories and to be aware of its presents. What is behind us [the future] cannot be seen and is liable to be forgotten readily. What is ahead of us [the past] cannot be forgotten so readily or ignored, for it is in front of our minds' eyes, always reminding us of its presence. The past is alive in us, so in more than a metaphorical sense the dead are alive - we are our history.

— EPELI HAU'OFA

1

THE HAPPIEST ISLANDS ON EARTH

Although 2008 was not my first volunteer trip to Melanesian, it was my first visit to Honiara, the capital town of the Solomon Islands. Honiara on the island of Guadalcanal was practically born from the United States military barracks that served as the headquarters during the infamous bloody and brutal World War Two campaign. During the day, it was a dusty town full of taxis spewing gas emissions into the heavy heated sky, creating a hazy layer of air that I was used to as a youth growing up in the suburbs of Los Angeles in the 1980s. Walking among the crowds, either going to work, school, the market, or just loitering, I wondered what the AQI (air quality index) might be here in Honiara. Nevertheless, I found Honiara an intriguing place with a unique vibe not replicated anywhere else in the world. The town is settled nicely in the south-western Pacific Ocean and is surrounded by an encroaching jungle. The jungle is like an unexpected snake silently and effortlessly swallowing everything in its path.

On this first visit, I was volunteering at the National

Archives, teaching a relatively young and inexperienced staff how to sort, appraise, and process a collection. Boxes of unprocessed material delivered from several Ministries were strewn everywhere in the Archives to the point where staff could hardly find their desks. The days were long, hot, and emotionally and physically exhausting. My colleague, Bernard —the Records Manager of the Archives at the time—and I would spend hours writing policies to help cope with this backlog of records. Bernard, a young man in his early twenties, had a keen interest in the history of the Solomon Islands. However, a lack of resources and funding made it very difficult for him to receive any formal education in the field. Instead, Bernard managed to learn from the volunteers—however few —that would venture to the archives to help. He felt it was his responsibility to clean up the Archives and was very grateful that I was there to offer my expertise in this endeavor. It also certainly helped that I did not mind getting my hands dirty working with the dusty and filthy records.

On one particular night after a long day at the Archives, Bernard called me from the lobby of my hotel asking if I wanted to go back to the Archives with him. I thought it would be an excellent opportunity to use the Archive's Internet to check and send email since there was no Internet at the hotel. I met him in the lobby, and together we made the short walk to the Archives. Typically I did not go out at night in Honiara for a few reasons. First, there are not a lot of things to do at night because the sidewalks roll up around five o'clock. Second, I felt it was just not prudent to be wandering the streets by myself, especially at night. God knows what vampires lurked in the darkness. However, with Bernard, it felt safe. Whenever I walked with him through town, it seemed that every person we met was his cousin, aunt, or uncle. I guess I figured that even the vampires were related to him on this night, and that was just fine.

As we made our way to the Archives, it was a balmy, sticky night. The air seemed very heavy, and the insects were humming. Sweat dripped down my face, and I could not wait to get to his office and blast the air conditioning. When we reached the property gate, Bernard stopped to talk to a group of men who were hanging out together chewing betel nut. When they smiled, the chew from the betel nut made their teeth look red as blood, as if they had been feeding off human necks. I thought to myself—*I knew it—vampires!* There was a sense of excitement among the men. A security guard then approached and joined the frantic conversation. The Solomon Islands have over sixty different languages and dialects, making it a very diverse linguistic environment. This group of men spoke in Pijin, the lingua franca, or common language, among the people of this island nation. Pijin was developed in the mid-1860s when the Solomon Islanders went to work, sometimes forcibly, on plantations of coastal Queensland, Australia. On this night, the men's conversation turned to a warning that someone heard a ghost inside the Archive building. Despite the men's supplications, the eerie news did not faze Bernard, who marched past the security guard and through the gate. I followed closely behind, wondering if I would have been better off staying with the vampires.

The National Archives of Solomon Islands are housed in a two-story building, which ironically looks just like a traditional haunted house. During the day, the building breathes a venerable yet creepy vibe, especially when the power goes out. This happened to me once when I was in the repository. It has no windows, and one can get a panic attack while stuck in the blackness and the stillness of the room. At night the building had an entirely different and chilling ambiance. As we entered the pitch-black building, Bernard fumbled for a light switch. The bulb was only bright enough to cast light in a three-foot radius. Heading upstairs, Bernard gave me more information about the ghost. Apparently, the security guard and his entourage heard voices coming from the Government Archivist's office at the end of a hall on the second floor. To the best of their knowledge, nobody had been in the building since the staff left at the end of the day.

As Bernard and I made our way to his office on the second floor, my flip-flops echoed throughout the stairwell. Once inside his office, we closed the door to the creeping darkness and took comfort in the room full of air conditioning and Internet. An hour or so later, Bernard left the room to have a chat, a smoke, a betel nut, or all three with the security guard and his entourage.

On the other hand, I grew more intrigued about the ghost only two doors down the hallway. Finally, I got up, opened the door, and entered the blackness. When my eyes adjusted to the darkness, I saw giant moths flying inside, which had entered through the windows with no screens; a gecko scurried along the wall. This alone would make any archivist worry about the safety of the records. But this was an unusual Archive in an unusual part of the world.

I crept along the hallway towards the "haunted" office as if I was a ghost and eventually came to the locked door. I placed my ear against the door. At first, I heard nothing. I listened closer. Then, I heard an undistinguishable THUMP and what sounded like a chair moving. I thought, Okay. I'm done for the night. I raced back to Bernard's office, grabbed my computer, and quickly returned to the safety of my hotel room.

The National Archives of Solomon Islands

The Melanesian region has some of the most beautiful landscapes in this world. Pristine beaches, lagoons, and waterfalls not inundated with tourists can be found in the interior and exterior of the islands. The markets are full of sweet fragrant flowers and pungent fish. There is a fascinating culture that is rich in history and changed by colonialism. The region also boasts of having some of the friendliest people in the world. In fact, the people of the Melanesian nation of Vanuatu have been called one of the "happiest people on earth" by the Happy Planet Index, which evaluates countries using four elements: wellbeing, life expectancy, inequality of outcomes, and ecological footprints.

Yet, after traveling to the region over a twelve-year span, I often felt there was something a bit more ominous, mysterious, and spooky that I could not quite see but could definitely feel. It is darkness lurking on the edge of a peaceful and exquisite environment. It is a hidden secret that people keep in the privacy of their homes. Author Rick Williamson wrote in his book *Cavorting With Cannibals*: "To the tourist who's visiting the Solomons for the first time, some of the islanders with fierce Melanesian features can look imposing. But even the meanest-looking local lived up to the islands' sociable reputation of being 'the happy isles.'" This stark and unquestionable contrast makes this one of the most intriguing places in the world.

Melanesia is composed of five island nations northeast of Australia extending in a southwestern direction. The countries in this region include Papua New Guinea, Solomon Islands, Vanuatu, New Caledonia, and Fiji. Melanesia has been the site of human habitation for tens of thousands of years. Today, about 12 million people reside here, and one can also find well over 1200 languages. Indeed, Melanesia is one of the most culturally complex regions in the entire world. Unlike their Polynesian cousins, Melanesians never worshipped gods. Instead, they acknowledged the spirits and other beings that shared the environment with them and recognized and revered their ancestors. Needless to say, the region has been a hotbed of study for historians, scientists, and anthropologists for the past several decades.

Explorers and navigators started to venture into the region between the sixteenth and eighteenth centuries. The Spanish navigator, Alvaro de Mendaña de Neira, set sail from Peru in 1567, looking for the fabled land known as Terra Australis. After approximately eighty days at sea, he thought he had reached Terra Australis, but in fact, it was the Santa Isabel of the Solomon Islands, named for the patron saint, that had guided his journey. Mendaña's voyage was perceived as a failure, and he received little praise for his efforts. Cyclones, low rations, and a dwindling crew forced him to head back to Peru, reaching Callao on September 11, 1569. However, those who later received word of his voyage and mapped his discovery eventually called the islands the Solomons. A four-star hotel called the Solomon Kitano Mendaña Hotel can be found on Mendaña Avenue in Honiara, Guadalcanal, in honor of the island's first navigator.

Mendaña died on a return trip to the Solomon Islands in 1595. His pilot Pedro Fernandes de Queiros eventually commanded another voyage in 1606, wanting to find Terra Australis and colonize the Solomon Islands and bring Christianity to the natives. Unfortunately, without the aid of charts, Queiros had trouble finding the Solomon Islands. After weeks of enduring dwindling supplies and a bickering crew, he finally came upon a large landmass, which he believed was Terra Australis. He named it Australia del Espiritu Santo. Today, the island is known as Espiritu Santo in the Vanuatu island chain. Queiros' settlement did not last long. It was hampered by chronic food shortages and constant confrontations with the natives. There were no religious conversions. However, there was a growing sense that this was not the great Southern Continent—that it was just another large island. Queiros decided to pack up the settlement and explore other areas to the west, eventually discovering New Guinea and the Philippines. The exploits of Mendaña and Querios may not be "the stuff of legend," but what they did was very important—they put the Solomon Islands and Vanuatu on the map.

Although more navigators would explore the Pacific Islands between the seventeenth and eighteenth centuries, none were as popular and controversial as Captain James Cook. His exploits and mapping expertise opened up the region, eventually enabling whalers, missionaries, and colonists to venture into these secluded and mysterious lands.

Sadly, those that followed Captain Cook brought additional issues, undermining the indigenous people in many ways—losing control over their resources and culture. This eventually led to the loss of sociocultural efficacy—they no longer felt they were in control of their destiny. Much of this is still felt today.

Cook made three voyages in the region between the years 1768 to 1779. His journeys have been well studied and documented by historians, scientists, writers, and avid fans of the subject. Cook kept a personal log, or journal, of the ship's movements and daily events, as well as an official log during his voyages. He was very interested in the places he discovered and visited, and his entries showed that he interacted with the natives without prejudice. Cook indeed wrote like a ship's captain. His logs were written in a very professional, methodical style, as though nothing really shocked or amazed him. Yet, it was full of detail, making sure to get all the facts correct. These logs were eventually published and would pique the imaginations of his readers.

Interestingly, Captain Cook was, perhaps, controversially indifferent about surveying the Fijian islands. Cook's biographer, J.C. Beaglehole, was surprised that Cook did not commit to this undertaking. He believed Cook's health might have been the cause of this oversight and wrote that Cook became more tired, angry, violent, and irrational during his third voyage to the Pacific. Beaglehole asked the question about Cook avoiding Fiji, "Was Cook beginning to experience a certain inner tiredness?" The truth seemed to have been more straightforward. While visiting Tonga, he was informed that the Fijians were warlike people and cannibals and that access to supplies would be difficult, especially for his livestock on board the ship. Cook did not want to embark on an extended and uncertain cruise around the Fijian islands with the uncertainty of getting his livestock fed adequately. Thus, he sailed back to Tahiti, which he knew very well.

Cook made a more significant contribution to the history and eventual colonization of Melanesia. On his first voyage in 1770, he skirted the coast of New Guinea, and in doing so, he learned the answer to a question that had vexed him for some time—was New Guinea a part of the mainland of Australia? On this second voyage, however, Cook tried landing on some of the Melanesian islands. In July of 1774, he sighted "Queiros's Land" named after Pedro Fernandes de Queiros. The islands were actually Maewo and Ambae of the Vanuatu archipelago. He would call this group of islands the New Hebrides. This name would remain until its independence in 1980 when the New Republic of Vanuatu was formed.

Cook continued to sail onward and found anchorage in a harbor on the island of Malekula, which is the second-largest island in Vanuatu, Espiritu Santo being the largest. He took a party ashore. When they encountered the natives in the shallow waters, Cook noted that he and a native exchanged green branches as a symbol of peace.

The natives would believe that Cook was a chief or a god, but on this occasion in Vanuatu, they referred to him as a ghost and addressed him as *tamar* or *tamach*, which meant spirit in the local language. On Erramongo in the same island chain, the natives believed that Cook was a dangerous ghost. Despite this, they were not afraid to defend their island.

A scuffle broke out when islanders attacked the approaching boat. Cook did not want to fire his musket on a crowd of natives, so he aimed solely for the chief directing the attack. Unfortunately, his musket jammed, forcing him to order his crew onboard the ship to fire their guns, killing a few of the natives, including the chief. Cook wrote, "These islanders are a different race of people to those on Mallecollo (Malekula)." He would give the name of the place Traitors Head "from the treacherous behaviour of the inhabitants."

From Erromango, Cook would sail to the neighboring island of Tanna before discovering New Caledonia. On Tanna, the active volcano, Yasur, was truly a spectacle and attracted the attention of Cook and his crew. Sulfurous waters bubbled forth in one place, mud boiled in another, and the sky at night was ablaze with the continuous eruptions.

Landing on the island turned out to be a bit trickier as the Tannese gathered in force, baring their teeth at them. Eventually, Cook anchored in a bay. After a few days, the natives gradually became friendly, sharing coconuts without expecting anything in exchange. Interestingly, if the Tannese had treated Cook and his men like ghosts, the peace would not have lasted as long. Cook's men became more nervous by the natives who kept their women at a safe distance and were always armed. Altercations between Cook's men and the natives inevitably came to a boiling point, and one of Cook's marines shot and killed a native. This incensed Cook because he always tried to restrain violence, but he knew it was diffi-cult to prevent it, especially in Melanesia.

A strange, new land was discovered in September of 1774, and Cook named it New Caledonia. He found the people on this long island less cautious and more curious than they had been throughout the New Hebrides. The natives approached Cook and his men without carrying weapons and made speeches, although the Europeans did not understand what they were saying. Cook was impressed with New Caledonia and felt that the island's "mountains, streams, plantations, little Stragling Villages, woods, and beaches, might afford a Picture of romance." He also noted that the women on this island, like in the New Hebrides, were far more chaste than those in Polynesia. Cook would chart the coastline of New Caledonia before moving out of Melanesia towards New Zealand. The natives of Melanesia would have no idea what Cook's exploits in the region would mean to the future of their islands. Within a hundred years, all five Melanesian countries would be colonized by four different European powers and one Eastern power. In 1884 Germany and Britain established protectorates in different halves of Papua New Guinea. Although the Dutch already annexed the Western boundary in 1828, which today would be Indonesia, the Germans settled in the northeast and adjacent islands, and the British claimed the southeast islands. The Germans saw more economic value in the land and used it to grow and produce coconut oil and cocoa. The British, however, saw little economic gain, and because of this, the culture of the native people in the southern part of Papua New Guinea remained almost unchanged well into the 1900s. This indifference eventually led to them passing control to Australia.

During World War One, the Australians took over the German-controlled portion and gave land grants to veterans in hopes of settling the country. This lasted until World War Two when the Japanese then seized control of large areas of Papua New Guinea. Eventually, with the Americans' help, the Australians would brutally and painstakingly drive the Japanese out of the islands. By the war's end, Papua New Guinea was placed under the Australian protectorate until its independence in 1975.

The British and the French were certainly trying to get their cut of the Pacific Islands pie in the Solomon Islands and New Caledonia, respectively. In 1893 the British declared a protectorate over the Solomon Islands and put a lot more effort into colonizing the archipelago. The colonial administration's influence would expose the natives to western education, Christianity, new technologies, and a filtered glimpse of the world beyond their shorelines. This would remain until World War Two, when the Japanese took some islands with little opposition from the British Solomon Islands Protectorate. The Allied Forces eventually pushed the Japanese out, and the British continued to be a protectorate. The war, however, did mark a new era in the Solomon's history that continued to influence the social, political, and economic landscape of the country. Not only did a nationalist movement spring up as a result of the war, but the indigenous population responded to attempts of decolonization as well. This put them on the path to independence, which was attained in 1978.

France annexed New Caledonia in 1853, hoping to develop a colony linked to settler colonialism, mineral exploitation, ranching, and the establishment of the penal colony. Things got off to a poor start between the French settlers and the indigenous people known as Kanaks. In 1855 settlers ventured outside their original settlement on the peninsula to look for better lands to cultivate. The Kanaks fought back, killing a few settlers. The French retaliated by burning villages and confiscating land. The Governor then enacted a decree and drew the distinction between occupied and vacant land, limiting the Kanak's right to occupy lands under cultivation. Thus, the "native reserve" was born, which the colonists believed would protect the Kanaks from losing all of their land. Then, to make matters worse, nickel was discovered in 1864, prompting the French government to establish mines, and encouraged more French settlers to migrate to New Caledonia to help run these mines. To the Kanaks, it truly felt as if they were losing their land. Revolts ensued—many of them. After World War Two, New Caledonia became an overseas territory of France in 1946. Tensions between the pro-French loyalists and the pro-independent groups continued to erupt well into the 1980s. Today, despite the resilience of the Kanak culture, New Caledonia remains a French territory.

With the British indifference in Papua New Guinea and the troubles the French experienced in New Caledonia, one would think that both nations would stay away from the rest of Melanesia. In the New Hebrides (Vanuatu), both countries set up a unique yet absurd colonial construct called a Condominium in 1906, where Britain and France governed the archipelago. The condominium was divided into two separate communities called the Anglophone and the Francophone. Thus, the 100,000 or so islanders, who were already separated into 110 languages, were divided into either one of these communities. Inevitably, this division created movements, revolts, and political unrest that would plague the island nation for several decades and bedevil constitutional progress. Jokingly it was called the "Pandemonium" because both the British and the French administrators ran separate police, education, and other services.

In 1958 an advisory council was established, hoping that land sales would be stopped and decolonization would begin. Finally, after 74 years of Condominium history, New Hebrides was given its independence on July 30, 1980, and to this day, the country is known as Vanuatu, which means "Our Land."

Fiji's road to colonization by the British was an unorthodox one. The British did not simply muscle their way into the islands but waited patiently to be asked to set up a protectorate. Chief Seru Epenisa Cakobau (or Thakombau) was a former cannibal who converted to Christianity in 1854 and renounced cannibalism. Cakobau united part of Fiji's warring tribes under his leadership, establishing a united Fijian kingdom. Sometimes he did it by negotiations. Often it was done through war, which was very similar to how Kamehameha I united the Hawaiian Islands.

Europeans had begun settling in Fiji during the nineteenth century, purchasing land from local chiefs for cotton and coconut plantations. The Americans personally held Cakobau responsible for an arson attack against the home of the American Consul and demanded compensation. More Americans in Fiji made similar claims against other chiefs asking exorbitantly inflated sums as compensation. Even the U.S. Navy moved into the islands and demanded payment of the "American debt." Cakobau had no other alternative but to make a deal with entrepreneurs from Australia who would pay the Americans in exchange for 200,000 acres of Fijian lands. This brought an increased number of foreigners to Fiji, which resulted in a land-rush and complete loss of law and order. Cakobau tried to fix the growing civil unrest, but it was futile, and he had no choice but to cede the Fijian islands to the British in 1874. Britain would rule Fiji for ninety-six years until the country became independent on October 10, 1970.

As I write, the world is in the midst of the coronavirus pandemic, and I am going on month number four of quarantine in my home. In my home state of California, there does not seem to be any end in sight, and the number of cases and deaths is still on the rise. Today is July 30, 2020, and I have been reminded that it is Vanuatu's 40th Anniversary of Independence. To this point, Vanuatu has remained coronavirus-free, and the Ni-Vanuatu have been gathering in the streets dressed in bright colors, waving flags, and swelling with pride. The country is having a nine-day public holiday. I am a little jealous that they get to party on their independence day while my country's celebrations were very subdued earlier in the month. Contrarily, working in Vanuatu's National Archives over the past decade, I saw firsthand how far their country has come. I feel proud that I was able to help maintain and preserve their history. During the celebration, Pastor Sethy Regenvanu, one of Vanuatu's original independence fighters, said, "We have always been independent people before white people came to Vanuatu. We were people who were living in our islands independently, depending on subsistence agriculture and our way of life, culture, and custom." The motto, "One people, one nation," is ringing throughout the capital town of Port Vila. They are very proud of their independence and will be for another forty years and beyond.

A sailing ship at anchor in Port Vila Bay, Vanuatu

———

In 2009 I made my second visit as an archivist volunteer to the National Library of Vanuatu in the capital town of Port Vila on the island of Efate. The library consisted of two small rooms on the second floor of the Cultural Center. It had one window and no air conditioning. Only two staff members ran the library. The two had the daunting and exhausting task of keeping up with the collection and the perpetual drove of school children and fieldworkers coming in to do research.

Anne, who was once a dedicated schoolteacher, became the Chief Librarian at the National Library. She was fiery, passionate, and indefatigable towards running the library on a small budget and a lack of resources. While volunteering to teach English in Port Vila during the 1960s, Anne fell in love with the country and decided to stay. She eventually married a ni-Vanuatu and had four children. Her husband was very involved with the independence movement but sadly passed away at a relatively young age, fifty-five.

When I met Anne, she was already pushing seventy years old and was already well past the retirement age in the country, but one would never know it. She was very active and always had time for her children and grandchildren. She was constantly saying hello to a passerby who was either related to her through her husband or who she once taught in school, which seemed to be everyone in Port Vila. One day I asked her, "So, has much changed in Port Vila, I mean, besides independence?"

"I used to canoe to work," she proudly answered.

"Oh, okay," I responded, wanting, perhaps, something more profound.

Anne then added, "And it's nice to see women wearing pants these days."

I thought about what she said for days. Of course, there has been change in this quiet, sleepy little Pacific town. Technology and transportation were constantly upgraded to make it safer and easier to get about on the island. The region was also very patriarchal. Thus, it was nice to see women have more of a voice, becoming more involved working in the different ministries or at regional universities.

Anne spoke three languages fluently- English, French, and the island pidgin, Bislama. Her youthful exuberance and infectious positive attitude kept things on an even keel during difficult times of changing protocols that the Ministry imposed on the library and passed down through the Cultural Center.

One late afternoon I asked Anne about the National Archives of Vanuatu and where it was located. Thinking about it for a second, she then remembered that the collections were stored in a house on the fringe of town. The head archivist had passed away a few years ago, and she had no idea who was overseeing it. I could see the wheels turning in her mind and a concerned expression in her eyes. The next day the two of us hopped in her little white Toyota Echo and made the trip to the archives. Unfortunately, the door was locked. Nobody was there to let us into the building. We walked around the building, peering into every window, trying to glimpse the conditions of the records.

It did not take us long to determine that the records had not been kept very well and had been ignored for some time. Collections were piled on the floor, and dust and dirt could be seen on the records. Everything was closed in a hot and humid room with no air circulation, which usually means a slow death for the paper items. To make things worse, the building was dilapidated and falling apart. Anne knew the importance of the archives and was not going to let these records waste away.

A few days later, she came back with a team of volunteers and collected the records. They took them back to the Cultural Center and eventually stored them in two twenty-foot containers. Not long after she collected the records, the house where they had been stored caught fire. From this day forward, Anne would wear a new hat as the Chief Archivist of Vanuatu.

The Vanuatu Cultural Centre, Port Vila, Vanuatu

One of the issues archivists of the Pacific Islands have had (and still do to a certain extent) was trying to prove the importance of the archives to the governing Ministry. A National Archives mission is to collect, preserve, provide access to government records, and support evidence-based governance. In the Pacific region, this would mean including records from all the Ministries and their offices. Sometimes, it would also include cultural records created by people and groups outside the government scope. The Pacific Islands were traditionally oral societies. Anne and I knew that it would be a real struggle to garner any support and resources for starting a new Vanuatu National Archives.

As we were developing policies and guidelines for the Archives' mission over the next several years, we received pushback from traditionalists saying that these were just "white man's" records. Perhaps they were, but they still told the story of Vanuatu. In his book, *The Shark God*, author Charles Montgomery wrote, "Melanesian history has long belonged to foreigners because the written word always trumps oral history. Through sermons and schoolbooks, the words of those early missionaries, traders, and colonial administrators lived on to shape collective memory."

It is a powerful yet truthful statement. Fortunately, as Anne and I would eventually learn, one could find precious records from missionaries, traders, and colonial administrators that captured traditional stories and customs. Anne had to postpone her retirement and make organizational changes to deal with the significant backlog of records in English, French, and Bislama. The Vanuatu National Library became the Vanuatu National Archives and Library, and she promoted her assistant librarian at the time to Chief Librarian. Anne changed her job title to Chief Archivist. Then over the next several years and with the help of one assistant and sometimes me, she painstakingly worked on establishing the new

Archives, which triumphantly culminated with the opening of the new Vanuatu National Archives and Library building in August 2013.

The word Melanesia comes from the Greeks and means "black islands" (*melas* meaning black and *nesos* meaning island). It refers to the dark skins of the inhabitants. It must be said that early descriptions of the Melanesians were not very complimentary. In 1774, after sailing from Polynesia to Melanesia, Cook was definitely taken by surprise by his first encounter with the natives in Vanuatu. He mentioned in his journal that they spoke an entirely different language than what he was used to, but also he wrote, "they are almost black or rather a dark chocolate colour, slenderly made, not tall, have monkey faces and woolly hair."

Other foreigners came along and tried to describe the Melanesian, often not in a very flattering way. In 1845 the Marist missionary, Bishop Jean Baptiste Epalle, was told that the Melanesians were "savage fighters, jealous of their land rights, suspicious of strangers and given to head-hunting and cannibalism." This is not exactly what a missionary wants to hear before setting off to evangelize the Solomon Islands.

Beatrice Grimshaw, a novelist in the Victorian Age, spent many years in Melanesia. She described the ni-Vanuatu (indigenous) in her book *From Fiji to the Cannibal Islands*, "The New Hebridean, in his native state, is neither more nor less than a murderous, filthy, and unhappy brute." She was a bit kinder in her depiction of the Fijian, "The Fijians themselves, tall, magnificently built people of a colour between coffee and bronze, with stiff brushlike hair...." Grimshaw felt that the Fijians were part Melanesian and part Polynesian and that the Fijian islands were the connecting link between the Eastern and Western Pacific. She observed, "East of Fiji, life was one long lotus-eating dream, stirred only by the occasional parties of pleasures, feasting, love-making, dancing, and a very little cultivating work." However, she was not as kind when defining Melanesia. She wrote, "Westward of Fiji lie the dark, wicked cannibal groups of the Solomons, Banks, and New Hebrides, where life is more like a nightmare than a dream, murder stalks openly in broad daylight, the people are nearer to monkeys than to human beings in aspect, and music and dancing are little practiced and in the rudest possible state." Ironically, despite this rather rude review, Grimshaw would live over twenty years in Papua New Guinea writing travelogues and novels, avidly promoting colonization and settlement, which she believed would bring real fulfillment and nobility to the Pacific Islands.

My immediate observation of Melanesia was that the region was simply tucked away in the corner of the earth, and it always seemed to me that the people of Melanesia were caught between the two worlds—a modern one of commerce and technology, and the other living in a more traditional way of life. To me, they just seemed more comfortable and happier when they resorted to their traditional ways. Sometimes I wondered what life on these islands would be like today if they were never discovered. Even Cook believed that once you enter the coil of civilization, you could not go back. After visiting Tahiti several times, he wrote, "I cannot avoid expressing it as my real opinion that it would have been far better for these poor people never to have known our superiority in the accommodations and arts that make life comfortable, than after once knowing it, to be again left abandoned in their original incapacity of improvement. Indeed, they cannot be restored to that happy mediocrity in which they lived before we discovered them." I believe the same could be said for the rest of the Pacific Islands, including Melanesia. They are "developing" countries that are still developing. They are not first-world countries, and I would not label them as third-world countries. They are not poor. They are never envious of others. They do not long for a better life. Their society is one of living with the land and sharing it with their family, and that is what is important in this world. Cook would question, "Where is the happy life?" The natives he met throughout the Pacific had every natural luxury and seemed to be happy. By contrast, the Europeans, with their complicated civilization, were unhappy. Perhaps civilization failed because it had abandoned nature. Unfortunately, one could not turn his back on civilization; "once it was known, there was no choice but to continue with it."

Be that as it may, Melanesia was such a paradox that intrigued me every time I ventured there. The people's beautiful and infectious smile would show their teeth reddened with betel nut as if they had been suffering from scurvy. I would amicably be offered a ride in the back of a pick-up truck only to see that I would have to share it with a recently caught six-foot crocodile (I said thanks, but no thanks). I would ride on a bus full of friendly folk but suffocate from the oppressive stench of body odor. There were idyllic lagoons on the fringe of dark jungles. Bats the size of eagles screeched from tree to tree during a short yet picturesque sunset. Something was just a little off, and I loved it. The shadows always seemed to want to tell a different story. Thus, during my stays throughout the region, I decided to look deeper into the heart of the culture. And, like the ghost behind the door, I could not help but poke my head out more inquisitively and pique my curiosity about this very eerie and enigmatic part of the world.

2

THE ROAD TO KASTOM

In 2008 I created the nonprofit organization Island Culture Archival Support (ICAS). Quite simply, its mission was to provide volunteer service to cultural heritage organizations such as archives, libraries, and museums throughout the vast region of the Pacific Islands. The idea to form the organization started with a volunteer trip to the Cook Islands in 2002. I spent three weeks there with the group called Global Volunteers—volunteering in various libraries throughout the island of Rarotonga. Having an avid interest in Pacific Islands culture and history, I enjoyed the volunteer work. Seeing the need for volunteers in this line of work firsthand, I knew I had found my niche. Most of the projects that ICAS got involved with were with the National Archives of the region dealing with preservation, processing, and disaster management of collections. On occasion, there were also some projects with Church and University Archives.

Although I envisioned having a hustling-bustling organization with a team of volunteers, it was pretty much a one-person operation with a very small governing board. Funding primarily came from individual donations, grants, and in good years, AmazonSmile disbursements, and was mainly used for airfare, archival supplies, and the shipment of these supplies. The projects were usually hands-on so that archival staff could work as they learn, or vice-versa. The hands-on model worked very well since the staff had difficulty obtaining any formal education in the archival field because of their isolation and lack of funding and resources. Eventually, however, the projects became fewer over time as I began holding workshops and speaking at conferences within the region and around the world. The tiny nonprofit grew into an international business.

Working in Melanesia was not exactly at the forefront of ICAS's passionate mission. I naively believed that most of the work would come from island nations of Polynesia such as the Cook Islands, Samoa, Tahiti, or from the Micronesian region, especially where the United States had their trust territories like Guam, Palau, and the Marshall Islands. The fiction writers of the nineteenth and twentieth centuries that enthralled me with their romanticized island adventures typically used French Polynesia, Hawaii, and Samoa as their idyllic backdrop. Writers such as Melville, Stevenson, Hall, Nordhoff, O'Brien, London, Frisbie, and Maugham, to name a few, understood the essence of island life, truly capturing its smells, sights, people, and environment. Non-fiction writers generally favored examining the issues that faced Micronesia and the Hawaiian islands. Indeed, they loved to tell and analyze historical stories such as the *Bounty*'s journey from England to its mutiny and beyond.

Though Melanesia would become a haven for anthropologists and ethnographers studying the many tribes and languages, the region just seemed to be a little misrepresented. To me, the region was developing countries full of danger and malaria. Jack London famously complained when he and some of his crew fell sick traveling around the Solomon Islands in his boat *The Snark* and wrote, "If I were a king, the worst punishment I could inflict on my enemies would be to banish them to the Solomons. On second thought, king or no king, I don't think I'd have the heart to do it."

I often chuckle at this quote whenever I think about it while working in Honiara. But I admit that it was the Melanesian islands where the mission of ICAS truly and unexpectedly began. And despite enduring illnesses, culture shock, and tsunami warnings, the relationship between the culture of Melanesia and myself would continue for the next twelve years.

During the time of the missionaries and colonization, the islanders of Melanesia (and throughout all of the Pacific Islands) were stripped of their culture and identity. As colonists moved into the islands, a system of servitude was set up for the islanders. After independence, the inhabitants had to learn how to govern themselves and had to recapture their culture. This brought in a whole new group of people wanting to give them a hand. Sometimes they were paid, and sometimes they were sent as volunteers. I often felt that many foreign volunteers who came to these islands meant well, but they had an assertive "you have to do it this way" approach, which the islanders often found a bit off-putting. Melanesians respond more enthusiastically and effectively to a collaborative approach. Author, Rick Williamson, captured the same sentiment when he quoted a ni-Vanuatu in his book *Cavorting with Cannibals,* "The Peace Corps, the teachers who are still working here, and the other aid agencies always feel they have to try and change our way of life. Some of what they do is good, but not much. We don't need them to tell us how to live."

Even during my first visit to Vanuatu, I could sense that what appeared to be a simple life on the surface was something more complex and more profound. It was something that I would never fully understand. In Vanuatu, this deep system of traditional culture is known as *kastom*.

Over the years, I have enjoyed reading the many authors who have tried to define the meaning of *kastom*. One of the best definitions comes from author Charles Montgomery in his book, *The Shark God,* which was about him retracing the steps of his great grandfather aboard the missionary ship, *The Southern Cross,* through Melanesia. He wrote, "*Kastom* is Melanesian history, religion, ritual, and magic, but it also refers to traditional systems of economics, social organization, politics, and medicine. If you say something is *kastom*, you are attaching it to the traditions of the ancestors." *Kastom* is a creole word from Bislama and English, derived from the Australian English pronunciation of custom. It also incorporates meaning from customary law, tradition, convention, and norm. It is something that tourists visiting Vanuatu will most likely not notice or probably will not care about unless they visit an actual *kastom* village. Even then, they will probably not notice these hidden traditional values and culture. Humorously, Montgomery also noted that the word, *kastom*, could be used as an excuse to get out of a question or situation. He provides a few examples: Why aren't women allowed to drink kava? *Kastom*. Why can't women be pastors? *Kastom*. Why don't kava bowls get washed between servings? *Kastom*. On one occasion, I wanted to take photographs at a ceremony, but it was clear that the men did not want their picture taken. They politely told me their reason— *kastom*.

———

While working at the Vanuatu National Library, Anne and I decided to take a lunch break and went to the market in the center of town. Like all the Pacific Islands, the market was the social focal point. It was where islanders came to sell their fruits, vegetables, fish that they caught, mats, and other traditional housewares and jewelry. Most things were quite economical except when a cruise ship was in port—then they hiked the prices. As we walked around the place, Anne wanted me to try the traditional laplap or root pudding dish. It was made by pounding various roots such as taro, yam, or breadfruit into a dough wrapped in a banana leaf. Then it was cooked in an underground oven called an *uma* with coconut cream and pieces of chicken, pork, or fish. It was one of those kinds of casseroles that if you saw it in a field, you would not want to step on it.

While we were eating, several people came up to her to ask who I was. Since her husband passed away a few years prior, it was against *kastom* for her to talk to me in public. At that moment, I felt like a million eyes were on me. I have always hated being the center of attention. I looked around like a convicted criminal in court, sweat pouring down my forehead. Our thirty-minute lunch seemed to turn into a ninety-minute lunch. Fortunately, Anne calmed me down. She simply explained to everyone who came up to us that I was a co-worker at the library. From that moment on, I was known as the guy who worked in the library. When passing people on the streets, they would say hello to me, and at times, surprisingly knew my name.

Kastom is not just a collection of rituals but a whole way of life that dictates almost all of one's actions and provides its own particular interpretation for just about everything that happens. Author, Rick Williamson, was an explorer and photojournalist who spent most of the 1990s and early 2000s exploring primitive yet unique tribes isolated chiefly in the highlands of Espiritu Santo, Vanuatu. He wrote about his experiences in his book, *Cavorting with Cannibals*. The book is fascinating, as Williamson tried to live and understand the *kastom* way of life. He believed that *kastom* could not be categorized into individual facets of life but encompass every aspect of the supernatural and natural sphere. He noted that he had to tread lightly when asking and receiving *kastom*, especially if it seemed like he was trying to steal vital parts of tradition. Apparently, under tribal law, the penalty to both a careless informant and the recipient of the most sacred of customs was death. While staying in a remote village in the Solomon Islands, Williamson recalls becoming sick with intense fever, chronic diarrhea, and bouts of vomiting. The villagers were very concerned about his illness and called in a *kastom* man known for being a traditional healer, but he was also known for the use of black magic. The healer first anointed Williamson's quivering body with lime and then spat a mouthful of chewed ginger into his ears, over his face, and on his stomach. This ritual was intended to drive out the evil spirit that invaded his soul. While western medicines drove out the illness in his body, the islanders were more concerned about the spirit. After this, Williamson's recovery was very quick.

The world of *kastom* was (and still is) full of spiritual and physical magic and wonder, all of which must be differentiated, contained, and controlled. It was never meant for anyone living outside the village. Williamson was one of the few outsiders to gain valuable insight into Melanesian primi-

tive villages never before documented. He learned the consequences while undertaking esoteric rituals and ceremonies.
He wrote, "*Kastom* demanded at the very least my blood must
flow and my bones must break." Williamson learned that to
receive information. He came to understand that with the
approval of ancestral spirits, closely guarded knowledge could
be gifted at the discretion of an individual but only if it was
reciprocated with a gift and only if the informant was confi-
dent that his people's wellbeing was never at risk. A world
populated by ghosts was a very different place than the ones
found in western civilizations. People in the west genuinely do
not think of the supernatural during their daily lives.
However, in the *kastom* world, the supernatural was not a
separate or unusual part of one's life but an integral and
essential aspect for which people had to take daily account.

One of the very few ways that people and tourists could
experience *kastom* was participation in drinking kava. Kava
comes from the *Piper methysticum* plant found throughout the
Pacific Islands. Melanesia, especially Vanuatu, can arguably
boast of having the most potent kava in the region. In Fiji, the
drink is also called *yaqona*. The kava roots are either chewed,
grated, or pounded into a paste and mixed with water
through a wisp or bark fiber, producing a muddy drink that
looks like a puddle on a country road. It has a very bitter,
earthy taste that can numb the mouth and induce a feeling of
relaxed passiveness. Traditionally, the drink was used to
communicate with ghosts and ancestors during cultural and
religious ceremonies. However, women and children were
never allowed to drink it. Why? *Kastom.*

Today, the rules on women drinking kava are a bit more
relaxed. I have noticed women having a drink with tourists as
part of a tour excursion. Fijian women are also consuming

more kava during special occasions such as birthday parties and family gatherings. Nevertheless, men usually gather at *nakamals* (meeting places), typically after a day's work, and drink together into the night—a practice similar to patronizing the pub in the western world. Nights of kava drinking inspire storytelling, gossip, making plans for the future, and relating the day's happenings. Indeed, a kava-drunk man will have very vivid dreams.

Researchers and scientists have been studying the therapeutic uses, benefits, and risks of drinking kava. It lowers inhibitions and makes people more relaxed and genial. One could certainly solve the world's problems in an amicable and mellow temperament. Scientists call drugs that have a relaxing, euphoric effect an anxiolytic drug, which is similar to alcohol, and thus, it could reduce stress and anxiety. Kava may be used as an alternative pain reliever instead of aspirin, acetaminophen, or ibuprofen. But like all things, when done too much, it could have health risks. It causes the skin to dry out, possibly leading to ulcers. Dizziness, muscle weakness, and vision impairment have also been noted in those who drink high doses of kava. Perhaps, most importantly, research has suggested that kava can be hepatoxic and may cause liver damage.

I recall talking to a colleague in Vanuatu about drinking kava. I wanted to try it, but my colleague was not amused by my eagerness to dapple with an unknown substance like a first-year college student. She had an unusually strong physical reaction to my interest.

"Are you all right?" I asked.

"My husband drank kava every night," she said.

"I bet he was a very relaxed man," I stupidly blurted.

"I truly believe the cause of his death was kava," she

continued, but seemed unwilling to go into any detail. I was very surprised and somewhat embarrassed. I certainly did not push it. I was just a moronic archivist that fell into the wrong conversation. I felt like I was the king of *faux pas*. This was just another inappropriate statement to add to my list.

Although research has shown that drinking kava does not lead to addiction or dependency, I did notice that many men in the region could not wait until twilight turns to night so that they could indulge in that intoxicating muddy water.

Kava experiences are widely told. Typically, a tourist will drink one or two shells and not feel much beyond the numbing of the lips. For those outsiders who are more involved with a Melanesian community, kava drinking can be a mind-blowing experience. One of my favorite stories told by Williamson about his *nakamal* participation was when he was staying in a village in Vanuatu,

"...because the kava was exceptionally strong no one in the nakamal could drink six shells. When he kept offering me one drink after another, I'd knocked back the previous five merely to be sociable, and had to force down the sixth shell. It wasn't until I ate a second piece of taro from the communal plate that the mind-numbing brew snuck up and suddenly grabbed me. The room began to spin violently, the ground wavered wildly, and my reeling senses became hopelessly bewildered."

Williamson shared that his vision began to double, his limbs became heavy, and every action was slow. He then began to vomit incessantly, and once this stopped, he "rolled around in a paralytic stupor" until the beverage sent him into a deep sleep.

———

In 2014, on my last volunteer trip to Vanuatu, the archives had two employees, Anne, of course, as the Chief Archivist, and Augustine, who was the Archivist Assistant. Augustine was an enthusiastic young man who loved working at the archives under the tutelage of Anne. The two got along tremendously well and fought the good fight in reinstating the Vanuatu National Archives. Together the two learned how to set up and run an archives building. Sometimes I would come and help out. I enjoyed working with Augustine. He was quite resourceful, and I can recall him using a wheelbarrow to transfer records from the container to the office in the cultural center. Every archivist in a non-developing world would gasp at the sight.

Augustine came from Pentecost Island and participated in the famed land diving ceremony, which occurs every year between April and June, and was a rite of passage for young males. It was also performed before the yam harvest to ensure a bountiful crop. Teenage boys and adult men performed this bungee-style jumping (called *nangola* in Bislama) from wooden towers 20 to 30 meters high (about 100 feet). The jumpers wear only *nambas* (penis sheaths) and tie specially chosen vines around their ankles. As younger males jump from smaller heights, older males make the death-defying leap from the top and can reach up to speeds at 45 miles per hour on their descent. They have no protective gear and rely solely on their bravery and the elasticity of the vines. There really is no margin for error for the jumper, and the ritualistic leap could leave the diver vulnerable to suffering severe head, neck, or back injury should the vines break. Although no official statistics are kept, the people of Vanuatu insist that injuries and fatalities are rare.

"The Leap of Faith," illustration by Tara Bonvillain

The ritual stems from a legend about a man who beat his wife. The wife fled and climbed to the top of a tall tree. The husband chased after her, and as he frantically climbed the tree, the wife tied vines around her ankle and jumped. The husband thought she had committed suicide. Filled with despair, he jumped too and died. As he was falling, there was no doubt that he saw her spring back up and past him. The islanders believe that the wood towers are home to spirits or some kind of deity of the husband. Women are not allowed to go near the towers. If they do, the deity will become angry and claim a man's life.

Augustine became the Chief Archivist after Anne's retirement, and by looking at him, it would be hard to believe that he ever tried land diving. Nevertheless, on my last week in Vanuatu, Augustine wanted to treat me to a kava ceremony. So on a Saturday afternoon, we met at the open-air hut on the grounds of the Cultural Center. Augustine brought a friend of his who was also from the island of Pentecost. He was the one who made the kava. The kava was strong, really strong. I was always a light drinker. After one beer, I could be seen dancing on the table. After three shells of kava, however, I was floored. I remember lying on a bench feeling groovy. I mean, literally, I could hear the Simon and Garfunkel song playing as I was watching puffy white clouds move majestically across the azure sky. "Slow down, you move too fast...." I wanted to grab the fluffy cloud and smother it like a pillow. Augustine was trying to tell me the legend of the kava. I only heard every other word. Men were the stalk, and women were the leaves —something like that. It was sexual. I think. It did not matter. I was numb, and the world was great. Good thing Anne was not here to see this. Augustine was beaming, proud of the potency of the Pentecost kava. In the end, he and his friend must have downed three-fourths of the kava bowl and walked away as if it was nothing. I, on the other hand, stumbled back to my un-airconditioned room. Fortunately, it was nearby. I then crashed on the bed and fell asleep to the rhythmic sound of my metronomic fan, and slept right through till noon the next day.

During my trips around the Pacific, I would partake in a shell or two of the earthy water either during parties or at the home of a colleague. Fijian kava was typically not as strong as it was in Vanuatu. However, during my latest trip to Fiji in 2019, a kava incident caught me by surprise. On this occasion, I was working at the Archives of the Catholic Diocese. One rainy Friday night, my colleague Katherine, who also volunteered at the Archives, and I were unexpectedly invited to the birthday party of one of the Nuns in the Sisters of Our Lady of Nazareth branch. There were about twenty nuns, and man did they party. After a hearty meal and cake, they brought out the kava bowl and began making kava, much to my surprise. I was in line when the first shell came to me. As custom dictated, I cupped my hands and clapped in a way that made a hollow sound and yelled, "*Bula!*" Then, I gulped down the swampy substance. When I finished the shell, the others in the room proudly exclaimed, *maca* (pronounced, maw-they), meaning, "it is drained."

After the third round of shells, I had to remove myself from the line. I was a little buzzed, and the rain sounded loud like rocks were hitting the roof of the house. The nuns started singing. I thought to myself— *this must be heaven.*

The fourth round of shells came to me, and I thought, *can I refuse it?* I clapped my hands and gulped it. A gecko called my name. It had the voice of reason like Jiminy Cricket. I wanted to apologize to the gecko. I saw the kava server dig into the bowl and scoop another shell. *Good grief, how deep is that bowl?* I thought. This time I had to refuse. When the shell reached me, I smiled, and held up my hand, and said, "No, thank you." The nuns looked at me imploringly, but I just grinned again and thought, "*kastom?*" As I left the party, they were still going strong. The kava drinking, the camaraderie, and the singing geckos continued long into my dreams that night.

Another unique part of kastom throughout Melanesia, particularly in Papua New Guinea and the Solomon Islands, is the Wantok system. Because there are hundreds of different languages in Papua New Guinea, Solomon Islands, and Vanuatu, the Wantok ("one talk" in Pidgin) system is connected to the practice of group identity and belonging, and caring for one's relatives. It is used as a term to express patterns of relationships that link people from the same families, tribes, islands, provinces, and nationalities. The Wantok system consists of a web of relationships, norms, and codes of behavior (kastom) that provide group security and stability.

A Fijian Kava Bowl

Perhaps, a simpler *"wantok"* meaning is that it is a comrade or friend with whom one has a close social bond and typically shares the same language. In traditional culture, the *Wantok* system worked very well. It bonded villagers together through mutual obligations. It was meant to ensure that nobody went hungry and everybody had somewhere to live.

Although *Wantokism* strengthens and solidifies relationships within the culture, it does have a number of issues and negative aspects. Politically, *wantoks* can easily force politicians to become corrupt and misuse public funds for personal purposes and gains. I can recall the happy day of receiving word that a grant application for a project at the Vanuatu National Archives was awarded to ICAS. I immediately wrote to Anne via email and told her of our accomplishment and asked her, "to whom and where should I send the money?" Anne quickly wrote back and told me not to send the money but keep it within the organization and use it appropriately from my end. I was a bit confused at first, but Anne explained her reasoning. She believed that the Ministries could get corrupt and misuse the funding. She had seen it happened time and time again. In fact, I can remember her exact words, "Brandon, if you send the money, we'll never see it. The money will be used elsewhere." I felt a little naïve. It was a kind of a wake-up call for me, but one I never forgot. Later, as I received subsequent grant money for various projects, I made sure to keep the money and not send it to the Ministry.

Another issue concerning those in a higher position and their *wantoks* is that job opportunities, or selection of employees, are not based on merit. Rather, it depends on whom you know rather than what you know. From a Melanesian viewpoint village, individuals who have more, or are in a higher, more prominent position, seem to be referred to as a "big man." The role of the "big man" is different than that of a chief or a traditional leader. This person typically denotes leadership, power, and influence earned through acquiring and sharing land or goods with his *wantoks*. Today, in Melanesia, good jobs are hard to come by. Nepotism fuels systematic corruption in terms of individuals using their power to give contracts to their *wantoks*, often resulting in appointing people for a position about whom they know little. The "big man" concept is also one of the reasons why the region was eventually evangelized. The islanders saw the missionaries, especially those from the region, as "big men." These Pacific Island missionaries permanently lived in the villages, rather than the European missionaries who often visited and left. As a result, their customs had a more long-term effect on the village people.

Reciprocity plays a major role in the *Wantok* system. It can be seen when people work together while making shelters, gardening, hunting, fishing, during bride-price payments, and land settlements. *Wantoks* think about the needs and wants of the community and are expected to share everything. The old adage, "you scratch my back, and I'll scratch your back," is very much entwined within the practice of *wantokism*. Charles Montgomery humorously noted this in his book, *The Shark God,* "If you have food, your *wantoks* will eat it. If you have money, they will ask for it. If you start a canteen store, they will clear shelves before you can sell anything. Clothes they will borrow permanently. If you join the government and move to a house in Honiara, your *wantoks* will move in with you and pester you until you divert some of that government cargo their way." If an outsider observes members of a village closely, they would easily get the feeling that some individuals were taking advantage of others from their own village or tribe, or family.

One example where the *wantok* system appears to take advantage of others happens during courtship and marriage. In the book *The Shark God,* Author Charles Montgomery told the readers about a person he met in the Solomon Islands named Derrick, who had once been the Casanova in the town of Auki on the island of Malaita. Montgomery wrote that Derrick "had fallen in love with the wrong girl. Her family demanded fifteen lengths of common shell money, two yards of red shell money, two thousand dolphin's teeth, and a whopping $6,000 in bride price, all of which was taking Derrick years to raise."

This little anecdote is a very common practice throughout Melanesia. One day I was working with my colleague, Kabini, who at the time was the conservator at the National Archives of Solomon Islands. Kabini was a soft-spoken yet ambitious young man volunteering at the Archives. Because of his devotion to the place, he eventually became a permanent staff member. He was beaming when he told me that he was getting married the following year. Although I had known Kabini for a couple of years, I never once saw him with his girlfriend. Everything seemed to be done in secret in Melanesia. "I had to save for quite a while," he told me.

"Save?" I was not quite sure what he meant.

"Shell money to her family in compensation to marry her," he said.

I nodded my head. Of course, he had to. Shell money is the traditional currency throughout the region and consists of beautifully carved discs of shell, which are then strung together. They can be about two meters (six feet) long, although pieces can be broken off to make lesser payments. Traditionally, shell money was used to pay for a dowry for a bride, land, pigs, and canoes. Shell money is an integral part of the culture and history of the islands, valued as much for its connection to the traditional way of life as for its monetary value. A man would need about fifty strings to give to a bride's family before he could marry and would often have to place himself in long-term debt to do so. I did not ask Kabini how much he had to pay for his bride, but she seemed worth every shell from the look upon his face.

A few days later, I learned that Bernard was keeping his relationship with his girlfriend a secret in fear that her *wantoks* would find out. One Saturday, the two of us were sitting at a beach south of the town of Honiara, watching a group of boys play soccer in their bare feet on a coral and shell beach. As an avid soccer player and fan, I cringed at every twist and turn the players made. *How on earth are their feet not getting cut up?* I shuttered at the thought of my prissy feet taking one step on the beach without sandals. Bernard, of course, was unfazed. If he wanted to, he would be able to join them. In the distance, about thirty yards from shore, the remnants of a World War Two US Navy boat jutted from the top of the surf. Every so often, Bernard would look for his girl-friend, who was with us but was swimming at the time. The waves seemed a little rough that day, and Bernard was making sure she was all right. He broke the silence and said, "I have to keep our relationship on the low."

"I bet that's hard," I responded. "You two seem to have so much fun when you're together."

"It's really hard. But, if I don't, her *wantoks* will want compensation."

A goal was scored, and Bernard's girlfriend made it to the World War Two wreck. "It's a cultural thing," he added with a little bit of a sigh. "Only a handful of people know we're dating." Bernard was not paranoid about getting caught with a girlfriend. In fact, I think it would have eased his mind. It took a lot of energy to sneak around a town where everyone knew each other.

"Do you watch who your sisters date?" I could not help but ask sarcastically. Bernard did not hesitate.

"Yeah, of course," he said.

The closest I have been to having *wantoks* of my own was when I was asked to play soccer with the Ministry that the National Archives of Solomon Islands fell under—the Ministry of Culture and Tourism. Perhaps, I was stretching the *wantok* concept a bit long. But why not? We were from the same ministry, spoke the same language (English), and had the same mutual obligation. There are approximately twenty Ministries in the Solomon Islands, and every year they have tournaments against each other in various sports. This particular time of the year, when I was there, it happened to be the soccer tournament. Soccer is a kind of international language of its own, and if you could play the sport, you always have friends no matter what country you are visiting. A few young men, such as Bernard and Kabini, who worked at the Archives, were on the team, and I was honored to be asked to play with them. On the day of the match, I went into town and bought some cheap cleats, which turned out to be a big mistake. After work, I felt like one of the boys as we piled in the back of a pick-up truck and headed to the field. I haven't been in the back of a pick-up since the 1980s. The field was right next to the airport, and we played the team from the Ministry of Women, Youth and Children Affairs.

Twilight moves fast in the tropics, and we barely finished the game before it became too dark to play. We won the game, and from that day on, I had a whole new group of *wantoks* who greeted me on the streets of Honiara. However, the next day, I paid for my cheap boots—I was suffering from plantar fasciitis. I could barely walk. Runners who have plantar fasciitis would understand what kind of pain I was experiencing. As I was making my way to the Archives during the morning, a tsunami warning from an offshore earthquake spread throughout the town like a juicy rumor, and people were scrambling to higher ground. That was the last thing I needed. I could not scramble anywhere except to the second floor of the Archives building, which was what I did. Thirty minutes later, I was relieved to learn that the warning turned out to be a false alarm. I did not take the cleats home with me; instead, I gave them to Bernard.

———

Missionaries and colonial and national administrators created various chiefs, including small chiefs, big chiefs, *kastom* chiefs, assistant chiefs, paramount chiefs, community chiefs, and church chiefs. This has diluted the authoritativeness and position of the chiefs, which begs the question: who has the right or obligation to manage conflicts? When a person becomes a "big man," it does not necessarily mean that he becomes a chief who looks after a community. Since the State has monopolized the use of force, chiefs are no longer revered for their supernatural powers. People are refusing to listen to their orders or come to meetings. Generally, the chiefs blame social changes like the increasing reliance on a cash economy, education, and the lack of respect for the chiefs' wisdom from the younger generation. This is particularly frustrating to the chief because the westernization of society with more attention on individual rights, and a materialistic approach to life, weakens the chief's ability to hold any influence within the community. Also, the fact that *kastom* laws are not written down weakens their power; many feel they need not obey what is not written. Villagers believe that chiefs have no authority under the country's constitution.

Although *kastom* is a social organization, economics, politics, communications, medicine, magic, and religion all woven together into a complex way of life and remains supported by those who live in the Melanesian countries, the system is currently facing considerable challenges for its survival. One respondent said, "the system of chiefs is weak, and we are afraid it will break." *Kastom* is not supported by the state, which poses problems in terms of conflict management. The chiefly system to control law and order, especially in urban environments, is not as strong as it once was.

Troubling signs began to spring up throughout the region. An example of this occurred on the island of Guadalcanal. After independence in 1978, men from the island of Malaita came to Honiara and treated the town as if they owned it. They took government jobs and ran businesses. Things came to a boil in the 1990s when locals blamed Malaitan men for a rash of murders. Guadalcanalese and Malaitans would clash throughout the town and its surrounding areas. This ethnic struggle would last until 2000. From the beginning of the conflict, the Guadalcanalese were convinced that "Malaitan *kastom* was not good *kastom*." More recently, in 2007, riots broke out in the capital of Port Vila, Vanuatu. *Kastom* seemed to fail the chiefs' plans to restore peace. The riots led to the death of three people because chiefs from the island of Tanna ordered a man from the island of Ambrym to be beaten 'till he revealed the names of the people alleged to have committed black magic. It was a mess. One chief was urging mobs to take action against the sorcerers, while other chiefs became powerless and found it futile to stop the riots. The *kastom* system completely broke down. With this last example, one can see that the main challenge facing *kastom* today is that the chief's role in the region has been diminished, making it difficult to administer any kind of authority effectively.

———

On the last day of my first visit to Vanuatu, I happened to be in the right place at the right time. Anne told me that I was lucky because I would see a ceremony that does not often occur in public. The Director of the Cultural Center, Ralph Regenvanu, was stepping down from his duties and going to law school. Regenvanu was a well-respected director with big political ambitions. In fact, he is currently the leader of the Opposition in Vanuatu, and I would not be surprised if someday soon he becomes the President or Prime Minister of the country. On this day, the party was not only celebrating Regenvanu's time at the Cultural Center, but it was also celebrating his becoming a chief.

Wow! What a party! Anne told me that I could have lived in Vanuatu for years and not seen anything like this. The ceremony started with ni-Vanuatu men playing the tam-tams (slit drums) as chiefs of the island entered and sat down in assigned chairs close to all the action. Everyone involved was dressed in traditional clothing, and they even brought out a pig, which made me a little nervous, thinking they might butcher it right then and there. In this part of the world, pig ownership and use in ceremonies traditionally conveyed status, wealth, and informal power. They were a cultural currency, and a person's status was often based on the number of pigs he owned. They also simply made good eats, especially when cooked in an underground oven.

The ceremony eventually moved into speeches. There were hours of speeches made by chiefs, dignitaries of the Australian High Commission, and co-workers. The speeches were interspersed with songs, and I was impressed with the

music my colleagues in the Cultural Center sang with such
beautiful, heavenly voices.

Becoming a Chief Ceremony, Port Vila, Vanuatu

After the speeches, the fanfare moved to the kava bowl
where Regenvanu, chiefs, and the dignitaries drank their ceremonial shells. Was this the moment that he officially became
a chief? Everyone else (men and women) were allowed to
have a shell or two when they finished. Then, the feast began
with mostly traditional food. It had been five hours since the
start of the ceremony. Everyone was famished and piled food
upon their plate a mile high; their patience was rewarded. I
ate my fill, bid adieu to my colleagues, and headed back to my
hotel to get ready to catch my long flight back home later that
night. As I left replete, I was pleased to see that the pig was
sitting in the shade snorting over clumps of grass, and for the
moment, life was good.

The pig during "Becoming a Chief Ceremony, Port Vila, Vanuatu

———

Another criticism of the *kastom* system is that women and youth are discriminated against by denying them a voice. Women's participation within their communities is either limited or non-existent. In some villages, they are not permitted to speak in *kastom* meetings, and if they are ever allowed to speak, they become too shy and afraid of being laughed at to say anything. In other instances, women talk, but they are not heard. There is even concern about how much the chiefs are prepared to help women with domestic violence and sexual abuse issues. Sadly, in many cases, the chiefs will only respond if the woman is seriously injured or if the beating occurs in public. Indeed, the region is primed for an equality revolution.

I was in the capital town of Suva, Fiji, looking for something to do one Saturday. A colleague recommended that I attend the 4th Annual National Women's Expo at the National Gymnasium. This event allowed women from all over the Fijian islands to showcase and sell their cultural artifacts and housewares such as mats, fans, baskets, sulus, shirts, blankets, embroidery bags, handbags, purses, kitchen utensils, soya-sauce, and other favorite traditional dishes. There were approximately 340 women from all of the islands of Fiji who set up booths to sell homemade items. If you are looking for a traditional souvenir to take home, this is the place to be. The Minister for Women, Culture, and Poverty Alleviation said the expo was an event to empower Fijian women as entrepreneurs and enhance their economic participation.

During the course of the three-day event, dignitaries and relevant guests made many speeches. Domestic violence and abuse within the villages seemed to be an important topic discussed by many speakers. It is a great start, as just a couple of decades ago, women were not allowed to talk about such matters. Today organizations such as Fijian Women Crisis Center support victims of gender-based violence through a range of services, including legal advice and psychological support. It also provides domestic violence prevention through raising awareness, providing education, and conducting relevant research throughout Fiji. Some villages elect women or have the chief's wife act as a spokesperson for other women within the council of chiefs. Her role is to link the chiefs and the women in the community bringing up issues that they want to discuss.

Despite *kastom* having negative issues in the modern age, it remains deeply woven within the fabric of life throughout the Melanesian region. It is the beating heart of culture and is passed down from generation to generation. *Kastom* is a complex structural way of living that depends on metaphys-ical forces and many other forms determined by strict tradi-tional guidelines. In Montgomery's book, *The Shark God,* the author interviewed a chief from the island of Tanna who talked about *kastom* and said, "The missionaries came and they told us not to make our *kastom*, but we were born with *kastom* and we won't forget it. My grandfather and my great-grandfather, they followed *kastom*. So, I will too. My life is easy. We eat, sleep and drink kava for free."

3

GHOSTS OF WAR

The ghosts of World War Two still linger throughout the Melanesian region, waiting for anyone who will take time to listen to them tell their stories. These peaceful tiny specks of islands were never meant to host the horrors of war. During this time, most of the islanders knew nothing about the outside world, with, perhaps, the exception of plantation experiences or the interactions they had with European missionaries, teachers, and colonial administrators. When the war crept a little closer after the Japanese bombing of Pearl Harbor, Hawaii, the Melanesians simply believed that this was just some kind of a "white man's" war. Very few islanders were able to follow the dramatic events taking place in Europe or hear the news about imperialistic Japanese spinning a web that grew larger and larger throughout the vast Pacific Ocean.

Today, the remnant of war can still be seen throughout some of the islands, especially where the fighting was at its fiercest. Allied ships jut from the water's surf, jeeps and airplanes stripped to the bare bones are scattered throughout the island, and old barracks stand rusting in the harsh environment. Dozens of unexploded ordinances are found, sometimes the hard way each year, and villagers are encouraged to alert experts to come and safely remove them. In Honiara, for example, The Explosive Ordinance Department (EO) of the Royal Solomon Islands Police Force has developed procedures for the safe removal of any explosives reported. Sometimes islanders have had to vacate their village for a certain amount of time until the EOD could safely remove the bomb or bombs. Nevertheless, in a region full of phantoms, the ghosts of war have added their timeless presence and continued their mission along the ridges of creeks, the sloping shelf of the surf, and the shadow of the jungles.

Although Fijians and New Caledonians braced themselves against falling into the Japanese web, they were relatively spared from the violent fighting between the Americans (with their Allies) and the Japanese. Initially, Fiji was one of the Japanese targets designed to seize French and British South Pacific islands east of Australia, which would have severed the sea lanes to Australia and New Zealand. This was the Japanese first step in effectively cutting them off from America. Because of the Japanese disaster at Midway, this plan came to a sudden halt, and Fiji became a support base for American Marines who would fight in the Solomon Islands campaign. An airstrip was built in Nadi (which later would be the international airport) to ensure the defense of the island. The coast was studded with gun emplacements. However, the Fijian Infantry Regiment was one of two battalions and commando units that saw service with the US Army. At first, they were focused on the defense of Fiji under New Zealand command. This command provided essential equipment, supplies, and personnel. Eventually, the Fijian regiment became more involved with the American island-hopping campaign and took part in battles at Guadalcanal, Florida Island, New Georgia, Vella Lavella, and Bougainville. In the Solomon Islands campaign, this regiment gained a reputation for bravery and was described by a war correspondent for their ambush tactics as "death with velvet gloves."

After the battle of Midway, the Americans had just enough naval power to prevent the Japanese from moving onto the French islands, especially New Caledonia, with its valuable natural resources of nickel and chromium. Before the war, approximately 1300 Japanese worked the mines and helped export resources to Japan. Not only did the island offer precious raw minerals, but it also possessed a harbor and an airfield. It is no wonder that the Japanese eyes bulged and their mouths watered at this strategic island location. At the time, the French and Australian defenses were thin, and once again, taking the island would sever the sea-lanes between Australia and America. In fact, the French considered putting a stop to the construction of a large airfield by the Australians in the vain hope that this would make the island less attractive to the Japanese.

Additionally, the Japanese believed that Australia would easily fall if they took New Caledonia since a vast part of its army was fighting in North Africa. But the loss at Midway delayed all that, and the American fleet steamed southward. By August of 1942, the capital town of Noumea (known as the Paris of the Pacific) and the southern tip of the island eventually became the principal American base for naval operations that were fought in the Solomon Islands and Papua New Guinea. Eventually, New Caledonia became an important rear area of the war.

In the spring of 1942, a Japanese invasion of the New

Hebrides (Vanuatu) seemed imminent. They had already pushed southward through Papua New Guinea and the Solomon Islands. Before the war, the British and the French Condominium government had continually been at odds with each other. Now, especially with the fall of France to the Germans, they had to work together more efficiently. Then around May, the U.S. Navy showed up at the island of Efate, where they quickly set up infrastructure and facilities. In fact, the island was thrust into the modern age with telephone lines, barracks, hospitals, and airfields. On the island of Espiritu Santo, the Americans constructed a major aviation and supply base the size of a small city. Remarkably, in just a few short weeks, Santo Island had three bomber airfields, two fighter airstrips, patrol boat maintenance and repair shops, a Navy yard, wharves, approximately 50 kilometers of roads, and an extensive telephone system. By July 1944, there were around 100,000 Americans stationed in Vanuatu, which doubled the ni-Vanuatu living in the islands. More impressively, approximately 500,000 soldiers passed through the islands during the war. Life in the camps got boring. The Japanese only managed to bomb Santo once, and the only casualty was a cow named Bossy. Other than that, men passed the time by watching movies, playing cards, taking hikes in the bush, and making jungle juice, which was concocted with alcohol made by illegal stills and mixed with mangoes or pawpaw.

The American novelist James A. Michener was one of those soldiers stationed on Santos during the war. The drowsy, enchanted Pacific island where the loudest noise was the rolling waves crashing along the beaches and the tranquil sun-drenched days dwindled into indigo nights radiant with stars enamored him. But war has a way of disrupting the serene balance of man and nature. Michener, who enlisted in the U.S. Navy and spent practically the entire war in the Pacific Islands, would witness this inevitable imbalance first hand. Like many of his fellow servicemen, he endured bouts of inactivity and melancholy. Fortunately, he enjoyed exploring and was always intrigued by different cultures. Michener often left the base and made journeys around the island. He was extremely fascinated with the indigenous tribes who ignored the military and continued to live their Stone Age existence. He loved the sounds that the tropical island produced throughout the day, such as how the palm trees heaved, sighed, and moaned. At night he loved how the jungle came to life outside his Quonset hut.

Michener's writing career began during World War Two where he was assigned to work as a naval historian. Eventually, he would turn his notes and impressions into his first book, *Tales of the South Pacific*, published in 1947. The book would gain him a Pulitzer Prize and later be the basis for the musical *South Pacific*. The fictional island that Michener created as Bali Ha'i was inspired by the mysterious volcanic atoll called Aoba or Ambae, which he could see about sixteen miles away. Although he only visited Aoba once, the island was a constant reminder that there were still places in the Pacific far removed from the war and where man and nature still lived in harmony.

Although Vanuatu was spared from the fighting, many lives were turned upside down, in a good way, with the American installations on their islands. The ni-Vanuatu found themselves working officially and unofficially for the U.S. military. About ten thousand islanders were conscripted on three-month contracts. They performed tasks such as unloading cargo, washing uniforms, serving as scouts and guides. Many worked as domestic servants for the troops. They were paid relatively high wages and were astounded by the wealth and the number of Americans in their islands. Never before have they seen so many men and the number of material goods in Vanuatu.

The ni-Vanuatu were also very impressed at the sight of Black American soldiers working alongside other Americans. The Black Americans looked like the islanders, and one could easily see why they were regarded as role models. They seemed privileged. The islanders were profoundly intrigued at how the racial line was bridged when they saw Black American soldiers and other Pacific Islanders doing the same jobs as white soldiers. They were amazed to see equality among the black and white soldiers, although they had no idea of the high levels of racism the Black American soldiers endured back home. This changed their local perception of their white colonial "masters" and the master/black servant relationships. The free and lax attitude the white American soldiers showed towards the Black American soldiers and the islanders were in stark contrast to the prewar British and French mindset towards them. Previously white colonials and missionaries were the only other foreigners with whom the islanders interacted. Thus, observing how the Black Americans were treated during these war years could be partly credited with the start of independence movements in the Melanesian countries of Papua New Guinea, Solomon Islands, and Vanuatu.

The Black Lives Matter Movement has been raging across the United States during the summer in response to the killing of Black American George Floyd by Caucasian police officers. The movement's mission was to work for freedom, equality, and justice for Black people and, by extension, all people. After the Floyd killing, protests quickly ensued and were followed by demonstrations across the globe. Signs reading "Black Lives Matter" could be seen practically everywhere. Unfortunately, the timing could not have been worse as people were supposed to be sequestered in their homes to keep safe from the Covid-19 pandemic. But racism is a pandemic too and has been for a very long time. While most of the protests were peaceful at first, many degenerated into riots, looting, and violence.

I recall the Los Angeles riots of 1992 when Caucasian police officers brutally beat an African-American named Rodney King. The policemen went to trial and were acquitted, much to the chagrin of everyone. This set off a six-day riot that spiraled into a real mess. Caucasians were dragged out of their automobiles and beaten, Koreans, protecting their storefronts, got into gun battles with looters, and set fire to buildings all over the city. By the end, sixty-three people lost their lives, thousands were injured and arrested, and property damage was reported to be over $1 billion. I remember wondering if the disturbance would spill over to me in my suburban home only thirty miles away. Fortunately, the National Guard came in and put an end to the unrest. I remember thinking, *where do we go from here?* The pain and frustrations that could be seen on Black American faces were so palpable and overwhelming. What could be learned from what happened in Los Angeles? What do we need to make sure this never happens again?

Twenty-eight years later, the racism riots have returned but on a grander scale. The protests are lasting longer than six days. I feel we might actually learn from history this time, and I am optimistic that the "Black Lives Matter" movement will make a difference, but at what cost.

I brought up the "Black Lives Matter" movement because of how the Melanesians treated the Black American troops during the war. The islanders had no idea what the Black American soldier had to deal with and, in actuality, came from a country where they were discriminated against and segregated. Yet, during World War Two, more than 2.5 million Black American men registered for the draft, and out of these, 1.2 million served in the military. Approximately 167,000 African Americans served in the U.S. Navy, initially as attendants and cooks. Gradually, they were assigned duties as gun crews and other capacities. In the Pacific Theater, Black American combat units included the 93rd Infantry Division, which saw action on Bougainville Island, Papua New Guinea, the 24th Infantry Regiment, ten anti-aircraft battalions, and one coast artillery battalion. About 17,000 African Americans served in the Marine Corps during the war, and were primarily used as support troops in ammunition and depot companies. George Watson of the U.S. Army was the only Black American to be awarded the Medal of Honor for saving the lives of his comrades from drowning after their ship was torpedoed in the Pacific Ocean.

Black American women also volunteered to do their part in the war efforts. Many of them became nurses in both the U.S. Navy and the Army Nurse Corps. Others worked in the factories building ships, airplanes, tanks or assisted with scrap drives on the home front. Sadly, at the conclusion of the war, Black Americans returned home and found the same socioeconomic issues and racist violence as they faced before. They still struggled to get hired at well-paying jobs, encountered segregation, and endured targeted brutality. Nevertheless, at least with the Melanesians, Black Americans were treated equally and were considered an inspiration to the islanders.

———

In the late 1980s, the Vanuatu Cultural Center developed The World War Two Project with support from the U.S. National Science Foundation and the Wenner-Gren Foundation for Anthropological Research. The project's goal was to interview and record men and women who had lived through the war in Vanuatu. *Big Wok: Storian blong Wol Wo Tu long Vanuatu* was published in Bislama in 1998 and was composed of selective stories. The project would prove to be a lot more than just capturing war stories from a group of people before they passed away. Lessons were learned in regards to Vanuatu's stories, storytellers, and storytelling. Many of the captured themes were the Black American military experience in Vanu-atu, the Cargo Cult movements, and the good and bad events involving U.S. Military soldiers and doctors.

Interestingly, the war brought many people together from different communities who spoke different dialects. Bislama was the appropriate common language for telling war stories. The wartime events were often novel and unknown in *kastom*. War stories differed from *kastom* stories because they remained personal narratives that were not yet adapted into oral texts and retold to future generations. However, like *kastom* stories that celebrated a famous ancestral figure's accomplishments, war stories also had heroes with special or magical powers. For example, one *kastom*-like hero was a man named Leon Giovanni from Santos who served as ships' pilots and guides for U.S. Military patrols. Local storytellers would recall his special powers. Apparently, Giovanni was able to make himself invisible and discovered Japanese scouts and spies that nobody else could see. As time went by, many war stories and songs have been passed down to children and grandchildren, which have become part of the village or community memory. Because Vanuatu is traditionally composed of oral societies, there is no doubt that these stories will one day turn into *kastom* stories.

On August 14, 1945, the Japanese surrendered to the Allies, and the war was over. American troops began gradually pulling out of Vila on Efate Island. However, on Espiritu Santos, the Americans seemed to be in a great hurry to move off the island. The military debated on the best way to dispose of the massive amounts of equipment from the base. There would not have been ample space for the material on the ships heading back to the United States. The priority was for the servicemen to return home. There was concern that returning with all the equipment would affect the economy. Many Americans would instead buy cheap used vehicles if offered the choice rather than purchase a new car or truck. The U.S. Military wanted to sell the surplus equipment at a low cost and sell a lot to people from Vanuatu, Australia, and New Zealand. Unfortunately, this sale hardly made a dent in the number of materials they had, and thus, they tried to sell the rest of the equipment to the Condominium. The French authorities of the Condominium deliberately did not act right away and tried to be tricky. They believed that if they did not respond, the Americans would have no choice but to leave everything on the island, and the Condominium would get it all for free. So, the Americans became impatient and lined up all the jeeps, bulldozers, ambulances, and other heavy equipment near the Segond Channel that stretched for about three-quarters of a mile and then dumped it all into the sea. This also included Michener's desk and typewriter. The place where all this stuff was dumped would be known as Million Dollar Point.

———

On a short layover in Port Vila, Vanuatu, I met a group of Americans who, like me, were making their way to the Solomon Islands. Although Fiji could be thought of as the central hub of the Pacific, the rest of Melanesia was truly off the beaten track. Typically American tourists do not venture to the Pacific Islands any further than Hawaii. However, I have noticed that over the years, Fiji has been attracting more and more honeymoon couples or adventurous families, especially during the summer months. On the very few occasions when I have met an American in this part of the world, it was usually either an academic researcher from some university or a diver. On this particular trip, I happened to be sitting among a group of about six enthusiastic divers—three couples in their early thirties. I wondered if they were all on their honeymoon. They were loud, and I could feel the excitement in their tones, knowing that this next flight to Honiara would be the last leg of a very long trip. At this point, it had been at least a seventeen-hour trip just from LAX. After some cordial greetings with a couple of the divers sitting near me, and as we waited for passengers to board the plane, I asked what brought them out to the Solomons. "Diving, man," one of the divers said. "This place is like the Holy Grail of diving." The group was ready to party, dive and party some more. I nodded my head and smiled. I have always done that well. I was never really into extreme sports, even growing up in Southern California, where it was the mecca for surfing, skiing, and skateboarding.

Their enthusiasm grew on me as a sense of reaching our final destination seemed to be drawing closer.

"We've been planning this trip for over a year," another bearded diver said. By this time in the journey, we were all sporting a five-o'clock shadow, and in fact, some of us had a thick black moss growing on our faces. "We're going to dive around all the wreckages of World War Two."

"Of course," I said, but then quickly asked, "Aren't those like graveyards?"

The divers thought about it for a second. I had not meant to be a buzzkill.

"Nah, man. They're part of the coral reef now," another diver said.

I shook my head up and down but then thought, *wait, what?* But before I could say anything, the diver asked me where I was going to dive. The question threw me for a second. *"Was diving the only thing to do in Melanesia?"* I asked myself. I guess I could have said anything like I was a treasure hunter or something. When my daughter was five years old, she thought I was Indiana Jones traveling to far-flung places and bringing back odd gifts. But I did not make anything up and told them the truth—that I was on my way to work at the National Archives of Solomon Islands. Right—now, I was a buzzkill. I do not think they knew what the Archives was, so that was another conversation. Fortunately, I am the master of brevity. By the time the plane landed, I believe they honestly thought I was some weird Indiana Jones type and that my job sure beats working in a stale office.

As I made my way to the Archives the following morning, I stopped from afar to watch the group of divers load all their gear into a van. It was a lot of stuff. I envied their adventurous spirit. For them, it was all fun and games so far from home.

They laughed and giggled their way onto the van. One of the guys patted his girlfriend on her butt. The morning was already hot, and I was sweating. As I watched the van drive away, a passerby spat his betel nut chew on the ground near me. I did not notice it at first. I was too busy thinking about World War Two wreckages, party boats, giggling women in bikinis, and asking myself, *what am I doing here? There has to be a lot more here than I understand.* suddenly, Bernard came out of nowhere and slapped me on the shoulder and said, "Bro, welcome back. Do you want to see the American World War Two stuff this time?" I turned to him and saw his big smile. There was more to do than just archives.

"Yes. Yes, I do," I replied. This was Guadalcanal Island, after all. Bernard warned me not to step into the betel nut chew on the ground—it was a massive red puddle. Gross. We then proceeded to the Archives.

Unlike Fiji, New Caledonia, and Vanuatu, the war came to the Solomons Islands. By May 1942, the Japanese had arrived on the capital island of Tulagi. They found that the colonial administration had relocated to Auki on the island of Malaita, and most Europeans had been evacuated to Australia. The Japanese decided it would be strategically important to begin construction on an airfield, known today as Henderson Field, on the island of Guadalcanal. They believed that this would cut off the sea route between Australia and America. Plus, they could then set their eyes on taking Australia. The news that the Japanese were building an airstrip on Guadalcanal was unsettling to the American military, and thus, in August, they sent the U.S. First Marine Division under the command of Major General Alexander Vandegrift to capture the island. The "Solomon Campaign" was underway and would mark the first time the two armies would lock horns on land.

The Tokyo War Office wanted the battle of Guadalcanal to be a quick, decisive victory designed to convince the United States to abandon the war and sue for peace. Instead, it became a six-month brutal battle of attrition. The U.S. Marines quickly captured the partially built airfield and then fought inland through the thick, wet, insect-ridden jungle. The environment was merciless. A Japanese soldier once wrote before he died, "There is no sympathy in the jungle." If a bullet did not find you, a soldier did not have to go far to come in contact with dysentery, yaws, blackwater fever, or other tropical diseases. Approximately seventy-five percent of the U.S. Marines that left Guadalcanal had malaria. After a series of losses, the Tokyo War Office ordered a new brigade of about 20,000 men. They were not ready to give up Guadalcanal just yet and attacked heavily fortified American defensive positions. The losses were beginning to mount. The Japanese failed to take into account the sheer difficulties they would face by going through a tropical jungle. Many men were too fatigued to fight effectively.

Additionally, the terrain made communications quite difficult. The Japanese finally retreated and withdrew the rest of their troops from Guadalcanal by February 1943. The American victory ensured that Australia would be safe from a Japanese invasion. Still, the Americans knew this would be a long war as they began to push their way through Melanesia and the Pacific towards Japan.

In August of 2017, Solomon Islands celebrated the 75th anniversary of the Battle of Guadalcanal. Although solemn memories of those horrific years hung in the air, the presence of the Solomon Islands as an independent nation and a pristine South Pacific paradise helped create a festive atmosphere. Visitors from around the globe that included U.S. veterans and their families, Solomon Islanders, and military representatives from the World War Two Allies—Australia, Great Britain, and the United States attended the weeklong celebration.

There was a special focus during the celebrations, and it was the pivotal role that Solomon Islanders, such as fishermen and farmers, played during the fight against the Japanese. Like the ni-Vanuatu, the Solomon Islanders also contributed to the war cause by helping the Allies. They formed a labor corps that would assist in such tasks as cargo unloading and carrying, building airfields, spraying ponds to keep down malaria, acting as guides, and even loading ammunition. At times these jobs were dangerous, exposing the laborers to Japanese raids on allied bases.

Perhaps one of the most impressive and unique duties that Solomon Islanders performed was a coastwatcher. These dedicated islanders suddenly found themselves in the middle of the battle and risked their lives, families, and homes. Approximately 680 Solomon Islanders served with the coastwatchers and provided crucial information about Japanese troop and ship movements. After World War One, a secretive national security network that engaged civilians residing in coastal areas of Australia was set up to report on any suspicious activities. This also included the controlled territory of Papua New Guinea and the British administered Solomon Islands. Thus, by December 1941, the coastwatching network was already established when the United States declared war on Japan. Lieutenant Commander Eric Feldt, head of the coastwatching network at the outbreak of World War Two, saw the area northeast of Australia as a "fence with many gates to guard." In the Solomon Islands, about twenty-three coastwatching stations extended from Bougainville Island to San Cristobal in the southeast. The one characteristic that coastwatchers had in common was that they knew how to live and fend for themselves in the jungle. They all had considerable knowledge of local culture, traditions, environment, and people. This knowledge was critical for intelligence operations behind enemy lines. They broadcasted reports by transmitting them via a more enhanced telephone system known as the teleradio that was developed by the Australian company, Amalgamated Wireless Australasia (AWA), and could broadcast more than 400 miles by voice and 600 miles by Morse key. The movements of the Japanese on any island in Papua New Guinea and Solomons could be transferred within minutes across the Pacific. As Admiral William F. "Bull" Halsey once said, "The coastwatchers saved Guadalcanal, and Guadalcanal saved the Pacific."

Another interesting duty that Solomon Islanders were tasked with during the war was with search and rescue missions. Islanders rescued many downed Allied pilots and stranded sailors. These rescue crews were often credited to the coastwatchers and scouts, but many villagers also had their hand in these missions. One notable rescue mission was that of the future United States President John F. Kennedy, who was commanding a patrol-torpedo (PT) boat. A Japanese destroyer rammed the boat tossing Kennedy and his men into the water. In the blackness of the night, he safely guided his men, some who were severely injured, to the nearest island, which was three miles away. Four days later, an Australian coastwatcher and his scouts found Kennedy and his men and led them to the United States base on Rendova.

Although Australians coordinated the search and rescue missions, islanders did most of the rescues. If an Allied pilot or sailor was stranded in enemy territory, it boosted their morale to know that the scouting network would quickly react.

Indeed, approximately 321 Allied airmen and 280 United States sailors were rescued behind enemy lines during the Solomon Islands Campaign.

One Saturday morning, I met Bernard at the National Archives. He and Kabini were going to take me to see a couple of World War Two sites on Guadalcanal. Unfortunately, Kabini could not make it. He was busy getting ready for his wedding and was probably collecting shell money for his bride. Bernard was able to arrange for someone from the Ministry to pick us up and drive us around Honiara. Our first stop was a few kilometers outside of town at a World War Two Relic Museum. A guide came out of nowhere from the main road, and together, we hiked until we came upon an open space in the jungle. It was mainly full of U.S. war relics. My first impression was that the artifacts must have been collected from throughout the island and put together by someone to make a few bucks. There were planes, artillery guns, tanks, and pieces of most anything military—simply sitting around and rusting away in the intense environment like unwanted toys left in the rain. The planes were gutted, and the artillery was hollow. Everything stood still, waiting for the jungle to claim it once and for all. The place seemed a little eerie, and I wondered about the stories these relics could tell, but then I thought that these items could have simply been surplus that was left behind. As we walked away, I happened to glance back, thinking that I would probably never come back to this place again and should get one last look at the relics. Amazingly, everything had disappeared as if the jungle, indeed, consumed it, including the guide. Where did it go? Where did the guide go? Does he just wait there until another tourist stumbles upon the collection? It was odd, but it was Melanesia.

The World War Two Museum in the bush, Guadalcanal, Solomon Islands

Our next stop was back in the town of Honiara to visit the World War Two Guadalcanal American Memorial. Since I was an American, Bernard was really excited about taking me to this site. As an American, I felt it was my obligation to spend some time where my countrymen sacrificed their lives to liberate the Solomon Islands and maintain the freedom of the United States. The memorial was located on top of a hill on Skyline Drive overlooking Honiara and the Mataniko River. During construction in the early 1990s, the remains of an American soldier were found. A plaque for the Unknown Soldier was placed in the center of the memorial. It was later confirmed, through DNA testing, that the soldier was U.S. Marine Sgt. John Harold Branic. He was killed on August 19, 1942, and buried on the hilltop. It was a serene yet solemn place that was cooled by an ocean breeze. Near the airport were rolling hills where many battles were fought. It also had a very unobstructed view to Iron Bottom Sound, the nickname given to the body of water where many American ships were sunk during the Solomon Islands Campaign. Bernard and I walked around the memorial; there was hardly anyone there. The vistas were quite amazing. They could not have picked a more deserving and desirable spot.

The American World War Two Memorial, Guadalcanal, Solomon Islands

"Over there is the Bloody Ridge," Bernard enthusiastically said, pointing towards the hills. I nodded acceptingly. There were a few hills, but they all looked the same. Bernard was genuinely into the World War Two sites. Not all of the islanders were, but Bernard accepted it as part of his country's history. I felt a little ashamed by my limited knowledge of the Battle of Guadalcanal.

"Over there is where the battle of Alligator Creek took place." I squinted and took his word for it. A gust of wind brushed away the humidity for a spell, and it felt refreshing. I started to drift away into a daydream staring towards Iron Bottom Sound. I remember thinking what a strange place for two culturally disparate armies to come together to slug it out. The war never came to the United States, and it only came to Japan in that thunderous last month when they surrendered. I cannot imagine what my countrymen must have thought when they breached the beaches and fought in this kind of unforgiving environment.

Today, as I reminisce this visit to the memorial, I wonder what our Guadalcanal veterans, especially those who gave their lives, would have thought about the country today. The coronavirus cases continue to rise in the U.S., with approximately 177 thousand people dead and canceling just about every summer festival or event across the nation. Meanwhile, the Black Lives Matter movement continues its struggle against racism and challenges inequality and lack of fundamental human rights for all people of color. The country feels like it is on the verge of imploding, and there might just be a unique kind of revolution brewing in the near future.

Nevertheless, at the Guadalcanal Memorial, I stared at the large obelisk flanked by two flagpoles with the American flag on the left and the Solomon Islands flag on the right, both blowing briskly in the breeze. The soldiers who fought here knew nothing of what our country has presently become, and that is a good thing.

The war continued through the Eastern Solomon Islands and to Papua New Guinea. These turned out to be some of the most horrific battlegrounds of World War Two. Stretching for over 1500 miles from west to east, New Guinea is the second-largest island in the world. Allied soldiers had to endure fierce Japanese armies, intense heat, dense jungles, and, of course, island-borne diseases such as dengue fever, dysentery, scrub typhus, and malaria. There were no roadways. Native dirt trails that were only a yard wide were often used as supply lines. The soldiers rarely got a break from the rainfall. Downpours routinely turned footpaths into calf-deep mud, which exhausted the men. One veteran said, "It rains daily for nine months, and then the monsoons start." It was another battle of attrition, where the fighting was marked by patience and persistence from both sides. The lush rainforest, high humidity levels, and stubborn defenders made a mockery of conventional military deployments.

The New Guinea campaign was identified in five phases.

The first phase was the successful Japanese landings along the north coast, which gave them a series of bases spread out along the tip of New Guinea.

The second phase involved two failed attempts by the Japanese army to capture Port Moresby and a defeat at sea at the Battle of the Coral Sea. These losses allowed the Allies to go on the offensive and push the Japanese back along Kokoda Trail.

The third phase, which began in the summer of 1943, was the taking of the powerful Japanese base at Rabaul on the northeastern tip of the island of New Britain.

In the fourth phase of the campaign, the Allies tried to control the northeast coast of New Guinea and Dutch New Guinea, which was intended to clear the way for U.S. General MacArthur to return to the Philippines.

Finally, the fifth phase saw the Allies mopping up the remaining Japanese troops.

The campaign was one of the longest of the war. Battles took place on New Guinea and its surrounding island chain that lasted from March 1942 to the duration of the war in 1945.

At the start of the war, the population of Papua New

Guinea was approximately 1.5 million people. Most of them had little idea of what the war was all about. Even though it would affect roughly two-thirds of the island's population by the end, the islanders displayed remarkable courage, kindness, and compassion. Some islanders said that the Japanese treated them with extreme brutality, while others believed that they were spirits of the dead sent to liberate the people from European rule. The Allies, on the other hand, often treated the islanders as colonial subjects. As many as 37,000 New Guineans were working as forced labor and conscripted by both sides, forcing them to be refugees in their own land. Many islanders involved in the war worked as laborers recruited by the ANGAU (Australian New Guinea Administrative Unit). They were recruited to be carriers, stretcher-bearers, road workers, airfield construction workers, and plantation laborers. The coastwatchers depended on the native people to provide them with supplies and to serve as guides. Australians came to call the New Guineans "Fuzzy Wuzzy Angels" for treating wounded and lost soldiers with extreme kindness—providing them with food and shelter even at great risk to themselves. As the war struggled on, the Allies trained the islanders as soldiers and formed special fighting units, which later became part of the Pacific Islands Regiment. These small units achieved special recognition for their knowledge of the environment, experience, and skills.

The Second World War had absolutely nothing to do with the Melanesians, nor was it ever anticipated or wanted by the indigenous population. Be that as it may, the islanders endured the harsh realities that the war brought and contributed to the Allied cause unimaginably. Today, heroic legends and stories have been created to pass on to the next generation. These stories honor those who bravely became coastwatchers, scouts, undertook search and rescue missions, conducted guerrilla warfare against the Japanese, and formed military units that fought alongside the hardest Allied veterans. The Melanesians were primarily loyal to the Allies because of their social obligation to the country's (mainly Britain and France) that governed them. However, the introduction to the American soldiers provided opportunities for interracial interactions that were completely different than during prewar times. After the war, Melanesia entered a new era where passionate individuals dreamed of a new political climate that would not only demand changes but would also recover the lost parts of their culture.

World War Two Memorial Garden at the Honiara International Airport, Solomon Islands

As I leaned on the immaculately painted white wall at the Guadalcanal Memorial, I gazed over the landscape at the roads, bridges, wharves, and anything that seemed like a remnant of the war as a gust of wind blew sweat off my face. Bernard proudly turned towards me and said, "Even though we knew nothing of Americans and Japanese, the war was actually the beginning of our independence. That's why it's so important."

A plane took off at the airport, and Bernard and I watched it as it climbed altitude into the azure sky and disappeared behind puffy white clouds.

4

TAUGHT HOW TO SIN

The arrival of the missionaries to the Pacific Islands began almost immediately after Captain Cook's return to England from his first visit to the region. They were actually one of the first groups of Europeans to follow the explorers into the Pacific. Their resolve to evangelize the islanders was long and storied. It was like a new playground had opened up, and every denomination wanted to swing into action to deliver its version of Christianity. About a year before Cook was in Tahiti, explorer Louis Antoine de Bougainville dramatically warned the Tahitians that "one day they (the Christians) will come, with crucifix in one hand and the dagger in the other to cut your throats or to force you to accept their custom and opinions." Although there was some resistance, Polynesia was the first region to be converted, starting in 1797 when the ship *Duff* carrying four ordained clergymen with their wives and children first arrived in Tahiti. Reverend John Williams of the London Missionary Society came to Tahiti in 1817 and set up a program that would use islander converts to carry their message throughout the region.

Missionaries varied in their attitudes to traditional beliefs and customs. Some were narrow-minded with absurd and often harmful rigidities and did not bother to understand the custom way of life in the islands. Others tried to convert the natives while attempting to maintain some aspects of their culture. It is also worth noting that the islanders invited the missionaries to preach to them in many communities because they saw the attractive association of Christianity and peace. They believed the missionaries were "sacred men" like captains of warships. Those that had little standing in their community were especially interested in Christianity because they could create a different organization of authority and prestige where they could advance themselves. The Fijians, for one, readily accepted Christianity because they already had a religion with many similar points such as priests, afterlife, and heaven.

The arrival of the missionaries in the Pacific Islands has always been a topic of controversy. Cook questioned his discovery of the Tahitians and strongly felt that they were truly living an idyllic life and had no right to be disturbed. Bougainville had also asked, "What possible good could be brought to these people by Christian civilization with its overload of guilt, its hypocrisy, its cold-climate strictures, its physical sickness, and its ambition?"

The different denominations that descended upon the islands also compounded the native's problems by regarding one another as competitors. The mix of churches was far from harmonious, and they often fought one another for control of an island. One of the first writers to visit the Pacific Islands, Herman Melville, was very anti-colonialism and anti-missionary. He noted that an outrageous crime had been committed. He saw no happiness for the islanders anymore and believed that missionaries actually taught the islanders how to sin. Always pro-native, Melville would also question why the Tahitians should be forced to attend an alien church, submit to a foreign government, and adopt alien and harmful ways of living. Nevertheless, by the mid-1800s, the missionaries had achieved precisely what they set out to do throughout Polynesia. They then turned their attention towards the more unpredictable, darker societies of Melanesia.

One afternoon in 2010, while I was volunteering at the National Archives of the Solomon Islands, I was working with Kabini, who had been hired as the Archive's conservator. As I was training him on conserving documents, an elderly Caucasian man wearing sandals, shorts, and a t-shirt that had seen some better days, walked in the room. He sat himself down at a back table, pulled out a laptop, and instantly began working with a photograph collection. Kabini did not acknowledge him. The elderly man's attention was devoted entirely to the collection. He continued nose-deep in the material as if he was the only one in the room. As Kabini continued with his work, I sat there wondering who the heck he was. I waited to be introduced. A few minutes went by, but nothing—just silence. I finally leaned over to Kabini and asked who the man was. "That's Bishop Terry," Kabini answered without even looking up from the document he was cleaning. "He comes in to work on his church's archives." I watched Bishop Terry for a spell.

"Which church?" I asked.

"Anglican. Go say hello. He's nice." Indeed, he was. Bishop Terry Brown of Canada was consecrated and installed as the fourth bishop of the island of Malaita in 1996, which was one of the largest dioceses in the Anglican Church of Melanesia. He was the first Canadian to serve in Melanesia as Bishop. On Malaita, he impacted the islanders' lives by enhancing human resource development and infrastructure development and helping communities achieve their basic needs to have better rural water supplies. Ironically, speaking of better rural water supplies during this visit, Bernard was having trouble coming into work because the water supply to his home was not working. He had to physically go to a community pump and bring water back to his family. Sometimes the basic needs that we take for granted can be challenging to come by in a developing country, and it was amazing how time-consuming it was for him to ensure that his family had water each day until his supply source was fixed.

Bishop Terry retired in 2008 and lived in Honiara, where he not only continued to support diocesan programs but also gradually became the church's volunteer archivist. During this initial encounter, Bishop Terry was meticulously preserving and cataloging photographs and photographic albums of the notable Australian photographer, John W. Beattie, who in 1906 traveled on the missionary ship, *Southern Cross*. He photographed people and sites associated with the many missions throughout Melanesia, particularly in the Solomon Islands and Vanuatu. He was also using a small space in the repository of the National Archives of the Solomon Islands building to store the entire archives of the Anglican Church of Melanesia. One of the positive aspects of the Pacific Islands missionaries was that, in many cases, they kept terrific records of their daily lives and commitments and informative records of the lives of the natives. These were in the form of diaries, correspondence, photographs, and journals. I took a keen interest in Bishop Terry's work, as I loved working with photographs. The majority of the pictures that he was working on were from the late nineteenth century. I told him that I could help him by donating proper, acid-free storage containers (among other archival preservation supplies) for his collection. Thus, a relationship between us was born. Later that day, the Bishop and I went and had an early dinner at a newly opened, chic bistro operated by Australian ex-pats. The restaurant was an excellent addition to a very limited source of food services in the town. We sat at a table, and I can recall that the Bishop appeared hot, uncomfortable, with sweat beading on his forehead. I thought to myself, *how could anyone, especially a Canadian, live in this part of the world for almost a decade and a half?* The occasion reminded me of author Jack London's surmise of the "terrible Solomons," when he wrote, "It is true that fever and dysentery are perpetually on the walk-about, that loathsome skin diseases abound, that the air is saturated with a poison that bites into every pore, cut, or abrasion and plants malignant ulcers and that many strong men who escape dying there return as wrecks to their own country." But the Bishop was full of energy, and I was impressed at how fast he ate his burger and fries. He talked about his work posting Anglican records to the Project Canterbury website, a free online archive of out-of-print Anglican texts and related modern records. He must have sensed that I was worn out from the day. Typically, the first few days working in the Solomons can take a toll on me. I found that the heat, humidity, and time-change could be difficult to get used to right away. But, on this particular trip, I was a little frustrated with the new staff at the archives. Bishop Terry sensed my lethargy and asked how I was doing. He knew of my work with the archives in previous years.

"They seemed to have forgotten the basic rules of

archiving," I said with a sigh. "They're still placing records on the floor."

Bishop Terry nodded, polishing off the last of his fries. He noted their struggle to get much done during the course of a day. "It's hard here," he said. "There always seems to be some issue that keeps them away."

As Bishop Terry eased my frustration, I thought of Bernard and his water problem at home. But, it was true. Every employee at the Archives had to deal with domestic problems during the course of a week. When they were at work, they had to deal with frequent power outages and faulty electrical equipment. There was never a dull day at the Archives. Be that as it may, Bishop Terry and I would become good friends over the years. I would send him archival supplies for his records, and he would enthusiastically tell me about the collections or projects on which he was working. During my last conversation with Bishop Terry, he was visiting Queensland, Australia, in the early part of 2020. Then, Covid-19 struck, and he could not return to Canada. Thus, he self-isolated and kept busy writing a thirteen-chapter book about the history of the Sisters of the Church in the Solomon Islands that would be slated for publication in 2021.

The European missionaries had a real struggle on their hand while trying to convert the natives in Melanesia. First of all, their rigid methods of conveying the Gospel to the natives and the dependence on worship was the initial cause of the native's lack of interest. Second, the islanders were very superstitious and engaged in spirit and ancestral worship. These superstitious beliefs would eventually become advantageous to the missionaries in their ultimate goal of converting the natives by including the spirits of God, Jesus, and the Holy Spirit into their daily list of supernatural beings. It did take some time to convince the islanders that the "white man's" spirits were omniscient. Third, there was tribal warfare and cannibalism. Everyone lived in a constant state of fear. As a result, there was great distrust toward one another and wariness toward the missionaries.

Furthermore, the natives did not necessarily want to throw away their belief systems and traditions in exchange for the Christian message. Islands chiefs were also unreceptive towards the missionaries because they experienced a loss of power when villagers embraced the clergymen. However, the missionaries in the Pacific Islands knew that for conversion to be successful, they had to persuade and win over the chief first. Thus, the strategy was to convert the chief first. He would then help convert the villagers.

The tropical environment played a significant role in the missionaries' slow start. Insect-borne disease plagued the region. Malaria killed more Europeans during this time than anything else. On his trip around the world Jack London, who never became a big fan of Melanesia, arrived in the Solomon Islands and debated with his crew whether or not to take quinine pills, even as they endured fever, chills, and diarrhea. He would write, "Everybody had fever, everybody had dysentery, everybody had everything. Death was common." Over the past few decades, much has been done to combat malaria. Malaria has declined because of the mass distribution of bed nets, indoor and outdoor residual spraying, and intensive case detection and surveillance. However, cases remain, especially on isolated islands. The disease still exerts an enormous toll, not only on lives but also on medical costs and labor. Tourists traveling to this part of the world are required to bring malaria pills. For some travelers, this could be a catch-22, as

the malaria pills can make one queasy and sick for the duration of their trip.

The missionaries also gradually grew frustrated with the
converted Pacific Islanders who became missionaries, mainly
Polynesians. These island missionaries often showed feelings
of superiority over the Melanesians and were at times
haughty and acted in an overbearing manner with the natives.
Sometimes the island missionaries had high status in their
own societies and assumed that the Melanesians would
understand and respect this status.

Both the European and the converted Pacific Islands
missionaries misunderstood the culture of Melanesia. It was
different than in Polynesia and was driven by *kastom*. In other
parts of the Pacific, the missionaries tried to determine which
native practices were harmless traditions and thus acceptable
to keep and which practices were fetishisms or idolatries that
needed to be eradicated. But with *kastom*, the missionaries
had a hard time separating the religious traditions that
needed to be weeded out from the broader realm of traditional
practices. In Vanuatu, for example, conversion was a complex
process, and attempts to separate religion from *kastom* were
doomed to failure because such categorical divisions do not
exist in *kastom*. The lack of understanding and appreciation of
the ni-Vanuatu customs put them at risk, and if they breached
kastom, they could be killed quite swiftly. The islanders
believed that the white man was either a demon, an ancestral
ghost, or a missionary trying to steal or destroy *kastom*. Often,
the foolhardy evangelist would brazenly enter the highlands
to only end up on the menu and become a martyr.

Like the ghosts of World War Two creeping about
Melanesia and rearing their unfortunate stories from time to
time, the ghosts of the early missionaries have also produced

their unforgettable grisly stories in the region. In fact, some of the most well-known evangelists of the nineteenth century met their ill-fated demise in Melanesia. One of these distinguished missionaries who would die at the hands of the natives in Vanuatu was the Reverend John Williams of the London Missionary Society (LMS).

Since the time when Captain Cook was killed in Hawaii in 1779 and the sensational mutiny story of the ship *Bounty* under the command of Lieutenant William Bligh in 1789, people learned about life in the Pacific and the great opportunities for trade, and the opening of a new area for the gospel. The LMS, founded by evangelical clergymen and traders from different denominational backgrounds, inspired these published accounts. In 1817 the LMS sent a ship to the Society Islands and Tahiti. Aboard this ship was John Williams, accompanied by his wife, Mary, and other missionaries. Williams first served in the Leeward Islands of Huahine and Raiatea. By 1821 he was making a profit of about £1,800 a year for the LMS from the Raiatean coconut oil industry. He grew restless and wanted to expand his evangelism to other islands. He wrote to the LMS and said, "I cannot content myself within the narrow limits of a single reef." The LMS headquarters turned down his request. Then, William's wife became ill, and they had to travel to Sydney for treatment. On the way, the ship's captain made a detour to the island of Aitutaki in the Cook Islands, where Williams dropped off a couple of converted Raiatean teachers. This would be the beginning of the evangelical expansion.

Between 1828 and 1834, Williams would travel all over Polynesia from the Society Islands to the Cook Islands, Tonga, and Samoa via a ship that he helped build called the *Messenger of Peace*. His unwavering motivation to sustain the ministry and create new opportunities for the Gospel, as well as his energetic daily employment of building houses and roads, fishing, trading, and farming, made him somewhat of a legend in his own lifetime. He rarely became disillusioned when faced with uncertain situations. The only time he became frustrated was when the directors of the LMS refused to give him a fleet of vessels that could have made it easier for him to carry the gospel to distant islands or to travel to new fields of work. In 1834, Williams traveled back to England to do advocacy work, including purchasing a suitable missionary ship. He would remain there for four years. He also recruited more missionaries, especially to work in the Samoan island group, had the New Testament translated into Rarotongan (for Cook Islanders), and wrote his book, *A Narrative of Missionary Enterprises in the South Seas*. While in England, he seemed to please everyone: the evangelists with his tales of missionary success, the merchants with his accounts of fortunes, and the general public with his daring stories of determination and boldness.

Encouraged by praise, confidence, and a new ship named the *Camden*, Williams set sail for the Pacific from London on April 11, 1838. Hundreds of people lined the bridges, docks, and wharves to bid farewell to this famous and intrepid missionary. He first sailed to the island of Upolu, Samoa, where he spent some time getting his wife situated at a mission station. But this time, he would not remain long in Polynesia and instead ventured, with a few Samoan missionaries, to the more dangerous and unpredictable islands of Melanesia. Williams was oddly attracted to this region and found the Melanesians "a dour and suspicious assembly, each village a law unto itself with head-hunting and cannibalism rife." This was what made evangelizing the region challenging, and like most missionaries, he was determined to meet this challenge.

Williams also learned of the atrocities that the sandalwood traders were committing in the region at the time. The sandalwood trade's boom first hit the Polynesian islands of the Marquesas, Hawaii, and the Cook Islands in the early part of the nineteenth century. After the trees were exhausted in these islands, the traders began to look elsewhere in the Pacific. In 1829-30 the traders eventually converged on some of the islands of Melanesia, especially Erromango, New Hebrides, which had an abundance of sandalwood trees. The sandalwood trade was a bloody business run by ruthless men who avariciously pursued large profits. The European traders and their crews were very rough and uncompromising men who often got drunk and fought and mistreated the local people. Reverend William Gill described an account that occurred on the island of Efate in the New Hebrides in 1842. He wrote that after the crews of the sandalwood vessels landed, the natives stood in the way of the traders gaining the sandalwood without payment. A quarrel then ensued, and nearly one hundred of the defenseless, unsuspecting islanders were killed on the spot. The Reverend gruesomely continued,

> "Alarmed at this slaughter, about thirty others of the aged and women and children, fled to a cave, there hoping to find refuge from the fiend-like fury of the white foreigners; but the white men pursued them, filled up the mouth of the cave with dry brushwood, a fire was kindled and kept burning until the groans and shrieks of the whole company of guiltless natives were silenced to death! This being done, the foreigners were left masters of the district; they cut down sufficient wood to fill their ships and stealing a good

supply of pigs and yams, they sailed away glorying in their shame!"

Events such as this one were happening when the Reverend John Williams' ship *Camden* approached the islands of the New Hebrides a few years previous. By late 1839 the natives of these islands, especially on Erromango, were already apprehensive by the approach of the Europeans.

On November 19, 1839, Williams landed some Samoan missionaries on the island of Tanna. He then sailed to the island of Erromango—the same place Captain Cook and his men scuffled with the natives about sixty-five years earlier. At this time, the island suffered badly at the hands of the sandalwood traders, where the wood was fetching £35/a ton in places like China. One trader commented, "It was well known that they (the islanders) had been often ill-treated by foreigners, and their shyness and distrust were attributed to that cause."

Williams went ashore with the captain of the *Camden*, Robert Morgan, and two other missionaries, Mr. Harris and Mr. Cunningham. After handing out gifts to the islanders, Williams and Harris walked away, most likely in search of water. This made the islanders suspicious because they feared that the missionaries would steal their food just as previous European sandalwood traders had done. Captain Morgan witnessed that Williams and Harris were sitting down, and the natives brought them some coconuts and opened them up for them to drink. He also noticed that the women were sent away, typically a sign of "some mischief." Then, Williams, Harris, and Cunningham walked up the beach and turned right inland, and Captain Morgan lost sight of them. Moments later, Morgan saw the three running for their lives.

Cunningham ran for the boat, and Harris fell while attempting to leap across a stream of water and was killed by clubs and spears. According to Captain Morgan's eyewitness account,

"Williams made straight for the sea, with one native close behind. Mr. Williams fell backwards, the beach being stony, and at that point, the native struck him with a club. A second native also struck him, and another put arrows in the body. I was unable to recover the body as the natives were firing arrows at the boat. The body stayed on the beach for quite a time before the natives dragged it off the shore."

Later, the natives ate both of the dead missionaries.

Another story depicting this same incident related that three of the Erromango chiefs greeted both Williams and Harris. One of the chiefs, Natigo, stepped forward with a stick, placed it on the ground in front of Harris, and said, "*nar*," which meant that the stick was a *tabu* line that the missionaries were not supposed to cross. But, Harris did not understand and crossed the forbidden line, which was all it took for the natives to become hostile. Natigo chased down Williams and hacked him to death in front of horrified onlookers from the ship. Perhaps ironically, in this account, Williams was not cooked and eaten because the natives believed he was some kind of god and were afraid that his spirit would seek retribution. When Captain Morgan asked the Erromangans why they had murdered his friends, they answered: "in retaliation for 100s of our people killed by the foreigners who came to cut sandalwood."

By the mid-1860s, the sandalwood trade came to an abrupt end. The price of sandalwood in China had dropped significantly. This meant that the traders lost their desire to deal with the inhospitable Melanesian natives. However, a new threat fell upon the Melanesians when thousands of islanders were recruited as indentured laborers, often against their wishes, to work on the sugar plantations in Fiji and Queensland, Australia. The labor trade was known as "blackbirding," and would be remembered chiefly for the kidnapping and enslavement of islanders by dastardly men who stopped at nothing to gain full cargoes.

During the American Civil War (1861-1865), the price for cotton and sugarcane rose exponentially throughout the world and became a commodity. European settlers and capitalists particularly in Queensland, Australia, decided to take advantage of the price and developed their own cotton and sugar plantations. The problem was that these entrepreneurs needed a large labor force to run and maintain the plantations —which they did not have. Additionally, Queensland was a very hot tropical place to work, and the settling Europeans had a hard time adjusting to the climate. Thus, the plantation owners looked to bring Pacific Islanders to Australia, especially from Melanesia, because the islanders were used to living and working in this kind of climate. The plantation owners then had to get the islanders from Melanesian islands to Queensland and thus had to hire recruiters to go out and bring back laborers. This transfer of human cargo then became a lucrative business in itself.

Although working on the plantations in the early years of this venture was backbreaking work where islanders would spend up to ten hours in the field, recruiters would use different tricks to entice villagers to board a transfer ship, such as handing out tobacco and muskets. Indeed, some islanders willingly left because they wanted to work in a white man's community, seek adventure, procure some goods, or even elope with a lover. But, more often than naught, the islanders were kidnapped and forced to go to Queensland. A well-known plantation owner named Robert Townes, an Englishman who immigrated to Australia, hired a labor recruiter by the name of Ross Lewin. Lewin became one of the more prominent blackbirder recruiters, despite the rumors of his questionable character and tactics to entice islanders aboard his ship *Spunkie*. For example, he often pretended that his ship was a missionary ship. This attracted islanders. Or he would ram unsuspecting canoes and then pull the islanders out of the water. Ironically, Townes once wrote a letter to Lewin describing how the recruiter should peacefully acquire the laborers. Townes wrote:

"In engaging or persuading these people, you must tell them exactly what they will have to do; that is, their chief work will be in the cotton fields, that they will have a kind master to protect them; that you will take them back in twelve months, if not six and that you will be on the station to explain and interpret for them; that they will be paid at the rate of ten shillings per month (over and above their rations) for the able men and others according to their worth and value... You must endeavour to keep the natives in good humour and friendly with each other; on no account allow them to quarrel or have any of their national disputes on board; keep all such quarrelling from them; if you find such unfortunately to take place, at once separate them and put up bulkheads between them. Take care none of the old beachcombers smuggle themselves on board with the natives."

One wonders if Lewin ever received the letter and, if so if he read it. Over the years during this period, the missionaries would despise Lewin and reviled him as a slave trader. The British Royal navy would incessantly pursue him and coined the trader as "the greatest man stealer of them all. "

Throughout the blackbirding days, many of the laborers suffered tremendously. They were given little food, dirty water to drink, and were poorly clothed. Many died from dysentery, measles, or simply from physical exhaustion. Many of the recruits had no idea where they were going, why, how long they would be away, or how much they would be paid. The Australian public was appalled when witnessing the isolated acts of violence towards the laborers and seeing the laborers arrive sick and dying. With such public outcry, Australia passed the Polynesian Labourers Act in the late 1860s to regulate trade and reduce the suffering. Unfortunately, this regulation affected little change to the recruiting and plantation practices, and the Act's jurisdiction did not extend to the Melanesians. The latter were recruited for the plantations that were developing in Samoa and Fiji.

Blackbirding eventually came to an end, but not for another twenty years. In 1871 an event happened that would bring the blackbirding trade labor to the world's public view. It would be known as the Carl Incident. Near Bougainville, Papua New Guinea, about 180 kidnapped Solomon Islanders crowded into the ship's (*Carl*) hold, tried to escape. The ship's crew was unforgiving at this revolt, and they used them as target practice with their guns until about fifty were killed, and twenty others were wounded. The seventy dead and wounded islanders were then thrown into the shark-infested sea. This atrocity brought a lot of outcry and outrage from other country leaders. A year later, the English government passed the Pacific Islanders Protection Act, which ensured the active implementation of regulations that Australia created in the late 1860s. The Australian government would then pass the Act of 1885, which stated that no more recruiting licenses would be issued after December 31, 1890. This would officially end the Queensland labor trade, and by 1906 all of the Melanesians working on plantations would be deported back to their respective islands.

There were some benefits that the Melanesians gained from the blackbirding years. Working in Queensland exposed up to 100,000 Melanesians to European settlement life. It introduced the islanders to an unprecedented supply of manufactured goods, liquor, and tobacco, which they felt they could not live without. Additionally, when the laborers returned to their island with goods and cash after their servitude, many of them saw their community status significantly increased. Another unexpected benefit of labor recruitment was the creation of a common language. Papuans returned speaking Tok Pisin, Solomon Islanders Pijin, and New Hebrideans Bislama. These are now spoken widely in the region as a local *lingua franca*, consisting of 80 to 90 percent English with a mixture of local vocabularies. To this day, Melanesians from disparate communities can communicate with each other and share an ethnic identity transcending traditional rivalries.

Like the sandalwood trade period, the blackbirding period also brought a distrust towards Europeans who would come to Melanesian villages, especially along the coasts where many of the laborers lived or once lived. As the missionaries continued their drive and desire of bringing the Gospel to the region, they had to be very mindful of the animosity from the villagers who were now ready to defend themselves, ensuring the protection of their village.

———

On two walls of the second-floor conference room of the National Archives of Solomon Islands was a hand-painted mural depicting significant events in the country's history. In the middle of the mural on the bigger wall was a large painted map of the islands, surrounded by smaller boxes that colorfully and vividly told the story of these historic moments. Whenever we had meetings in this room, I could not help but stare at the pictures and lose myself within them. I have always been a daydreamer—which occasionally caused problems for me as a student. Sometimes I had to sit with my back to the mural to ensure that I remained focused and acted professionally during a meeting. Even then, I would find myself looking over my shoulder. There was something about the paintings. I could not stop myself from staring. Each square showed a pivotal historic moment such as blackbirding, the signing of Independence, World War Two, the Ethnic Tension, the Arrival of RAMSI, etc. I remember thinking that many of these famous occasions were created or impacted by the "white man" and wondered what kind of a country the Solomon Islands would be today if the explorers, traders, and missionaries had not influenced the people of these islands. Would these islands even be a country?

As I sat in meetings, there were times when we would discuss preserving the oldest records in the archives, which were early colonial records created by "white men." On a few occasions, while promoting my non-profit organization, a person of Pacific descent would come to me and ask, "Why would we want to preserve the *white man's* records?" I would usually explain that regardless of it being the "white man's" record, it was still part of the country's history and still needed to be archived. What about pre-colonial records? Ah! Like the rest of the Pacific Islands, the traditional records were passed down orally from generation to generation. If anything, the mural reminded me of the importance of capturing traditional records whenever possible. This might be a film recording a traditional dance, the method of building a canoe, or the teaching of a language. These are the kinds of records that keep culture alive. And in this volatile region that seemed to be very sensitive to globalization and the incessant pressures of modern technology, it remains even more critical to preserve the Melanesian cultural identity.

In the bottom left-hand corner of the mural is a box depicting a painting with the caption, "Killing of Bishop Patteson." This painting had always piqued my curiosity mainly because, at first, I had no idea who Bishop Patteson was. I thought that the word "Killing" was a strong word to use in such a setting. Perhaps, the word "death" or "end" would have been more appropriate. However, after learning more about him, I could understand that, like the Reverend John Williams, he was truly "killed" unexpectedly by natives.

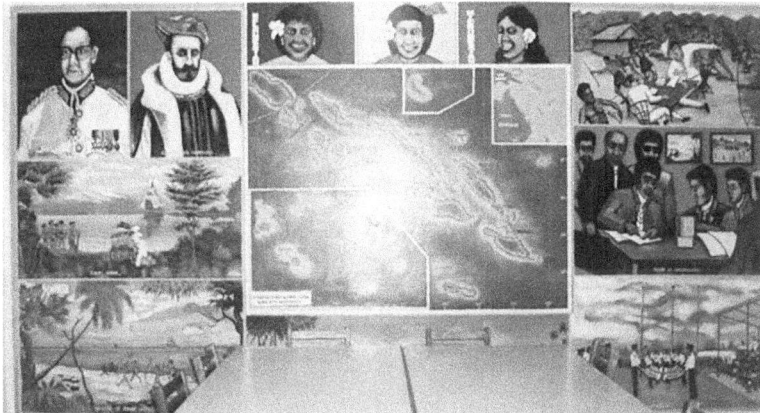

The Mural at the National Archives of Solomon Islands

Bishop John Coleridge Patteson was born in London, England, in 1827, grew up in Devon, and studied at Eton College and Balliol College in Oxford. When he was in his teens, he became heavily influenced by a sermon delivered by George Agustus Selwyn, who would become the first Anglican Bishop of New Zealand.

In 1855 Selwyn was back in England raising funds for his work that included Melanesia. He was also looking for associates that would help him manage his large diocese. While in England, Selwyn once again impressed Patteson with his adventures in New Zealand and Melanesia, and the two formed a strong friendship. In fact, Selwyn became a mentor to the young Patteson, who learned about the challenges of taking the Gospel to Melanesia and how the multiplicity of languages was a major hurdle. When Patteson was asked to help in the mission in Melanesia, he heartily accepted. On July 6, 1855, Selwyn and Patteson set sail to New Zealand.

Patteson had the gift of learning languages. He spoke German, Hebrew, and Arabic, and on the long passage to this relatively new world, he learned Maori, which was the native tongue of New Zealand. A year later, Selwyn took Patteson on his first tour of Melanesia, where the goal was to recruit islander boys and bring them to New Zealand for evangelical training. The two treated the islanders differently than most missionaries. Neither of them wanted to discriminate between the Melanesian and the European and believed the Melanesian customs should be retained within the tradition of the church. Patteson worked hard, long hours at the school in New Zealand, rapidly developing conversions. He would not accept a boy into the Christian faith until he was convinced that the boy was sincere. Eventually, the school would move to Norfolk Island, and Patteson would work there for the next five years. On February 24, 1861, at the age of thirty-four, he would be consecrated the first Bishop of Melanesia.

For the next ten years, John Coleridge Patteson would work throughout the islands of Melanesia and established a headquarters on the island of Mota in the Banks Group in Vanuatu. At this time, the blackbirding trade was in full swing. Initially, Patteson believed that the trade would be a potential benefit for his islanders. He thought they might benefit from an opportunity in a world that was quite different from their own. However, he was in favor of some labor recruitment regulations. He inevitably began to witness the disturbing methods in which the natives were being tricked, and he condemned the kidnapping of islanders. He wrote letters to influential people, as well as reporting it in the Anglican monthly *Mission Life*, writing how labor ships "greatly increased risk to himself and those with him." The British Navy, who loosely patrolled the region, could severely punish islanders deemed to endanger European lives. Still, when dealing with the blackbirders, the naval officers seemed to have little influence. The situation in Melanesia was becoming crucial as islanders began to act more hostile towards all white men, including the missionaries.

Patteson was never one to rest on his laurels and continued to work actively, despite health issues. On April 27, 1871, he set sail to other islands in Melanesia on the famous mission ship, *Southern Cross*. He traveled against the supplications of other bishops in New Zealand who begged Patteson to remain in his headquarters and rest. Unknown to him, this would be his last voyage. Just before eleven o'clock in the morning on September 21, 1871, the *Southern Cross* approached the quaint-sounding island of Nukapu in the Eastern Solomon Islands. Patteson had visited this island before with Bishop Selwyn and felt comfortable in the village. Around eleven thirty, the ship's boat was lowered, and in it were Bishop Patteson, Reverend Joseph Atkin, and three islander missionaries named Stephen, James, and John.

When the boat reached the reef, natives in several canoes met them. Because the tide was out, the boat could not make it to shore. Patteson transferred into one of the canoes and was taken to the beach while the rest of his companions remained in the boat and waited for him. As the missionaries waited for Patteson, three native canoes approached the vessel and asked the men where they came from. They told them that they came from New Zealand, Bauro, and Mota. Then, inexplicably as the canoes began to drift away from the boat, the natives fired a hail of arrows into the boat, hitting three of the four men. James threw himself on the bottom of the boat and escaped unhurt. Despite their injuries, the men managed to row back to the safety of the ship. Everyone on board wondered about the fate of Patteson. Although Atkin was fatally wounded, he insisted on taking the boat with four heavily armed companions to the island to look for the Bishop. When the boat returned to the *Southern Cross*, Reverend C. H. Brooke noted that a boat pulled a canoe with a bundle heaped in the middle. The heap was the body of Bishop Patteson. Brooke would write,

> "Yes, our Bishop's body, wrapped carefully in native matting, and tied at the neck and ancles. A palm frond was thrust into the breast, in which were five knots tied- the number of the slain, as they supposed, or possibly of those whom his death was meant to avenge. On removing the

matting, we found the right side of the skull completely shattered. The top of the head was cloven with some sharp weapon, and there were numerous arrow-wounds about the body."

On the following day, Joseph Atkin, who would later die along with Stephen Taroniara from their wounds, solemnly performed a service and buried the Bishop at sea.

The one gruesome fact that everyone agreed on was that Bishop Patteson died from his head being battered to pieces by a blunt object. But what actually occurred on the island that led to the killing was, and still is, under speculation and remains to be a topic of debate. The leading theory points toward an islander named Tetuli (also spelled—Teadule, Teatule) as the one who murdered the Bishop in vengeance of blackbirders taking five islanders including his nephew (or son, or father) just days before the arrival of Patteson. Tetuli made up his mind to kill the first white man who landed on the island. While the Bishop was resting on a mat, Tetuli quietly approached him with a heavy club and bashed his head. The natives wanted to take the body to the other side of the village for burial in a cemetery. They put the body in a canoe and placed a coconut leaf with knots tied in it on Patteson's chest as a charm to prevent the Bishop's soul from returning and haunting them. An islander (usually a woman) got into another canoe and began to tow the canoe with Patteson's body to the cemetery. On her way, she noticed Atkin's boat, got scared, and cast off, leaving the body to be picked up by Atkin. It was one of those stories that if you asked ten people, you would get ten different versions.

Nevertheless, the death of Patteson created an uproar in England and even drew a eulogy from Queen Victoria. The number of volunteer missionaries ready to leave for the Pacific Islands increased. About a year later, the Government passed the Pacific Islanders Protection Act that provided some sort of justice for islanders sold into slavery. Blackbirding did not end with the death of Bishop Patteson, but it started to draw a lot more attention that would eventually lead to its demise.

Even though many early explorers were from Catholic countries, the Catholic missionaries slowly started in the Pacific Islands region. These explorers did try to encourage Catholic authorities to consider sending missionaries to the islands, but it was not until 1822 that the church began to take action. The Protestant missionaries spreading the Gospel in the region were from Britain, while the first Catholic missionaries were French. Eventually, this would create a competitive environment where two denominations would persuade their subjects to follow their beliefs. It was not about the Gospel anymore.

In 1825 a few Catholic priests from the Société of Pipcus, or the Congregation du Sacre-Coeur de Jesus et de Marie based in Paris, traveled to Hawaii but were quickly expelled from representatives of the already well-rooted American Board of Missions. But the Catholics did not give up. Backed by a revival of faith following the Napoleonic wars and venturous trading organizations such as the Société de l'Oceanie who provided free passage to missionaries, Catholic missionaries got a foothold in the Gambier Islands Group of today's French Polynesia. However, it was not until about 1836 when, perhaps arguably, the most prolific and determined Catholic organization- the Société de Marie, better known as the Marists, thought about evangelizing islands west of the Cook Islands.

The Marists were under the leadership of Jean-Claude

Colin, who was determined to spread the Catholic faith throughout Oceania, despite never stepping one foot on an island. He orchestrated his plans from France and sent the first band of priests led by Bishop Jean Baptiste Pompallier to the Pacific. During this voyage, Pompallier left missionaries on the islands of Wallis and Futuna before making his headquarters in New Zealand. Although the Marists were successful in some parts of Polynesia, Colin was not very impressed with the way Pompallier was handling his duties in the Pacific. Some of the missionaries were starving and poorly administered. In 1842 one of Pompallier's priests, Jean-Baptiste Epalle, returned to Europe from New Zealand criticizing the actions of his superior. Colin and Epalle then went to Rome to present a plan for missionary activities in Melanesia and Micronesia and pointed out that Europeans had not yet corrupted these areas. Rome approved their plan and consecrated Epalle as the Bishop in charge. He departed London for the Pacific on February 2, 1845, reaching Sydney on June 22nd. Little did he imagine that he would become one of the first, if not the most regarded, Catholic martyr by the end of the year.

Bishop Epalle wanted his headquarters to be based in the Solomon Islands. He did not know much about the Melanesians and had only read reports that they were "more dour than the extrovert Polynesians, were savage fighters, jealous of their land rights, suspicious of strangers and given to headhunting." This was not exactly the glowing review he hoped for—not that it would have changed his mind anyway. He sailed to New Caledonia, San Cristobal Island, and then to Santa Ysabel Island, where he found the islanders friendly and ready to trade aboard the ship. After three days, Epalle decided to land. He was warned not to proceed any farther than Maunga Point. The natives there were enemies of the islanders that Epalle had been trading with aboard his ship. On December 16, Epalle underestimated this feud and led his party to the dangerous territory despite the warnings. He was met by a large group of the Maunga tribe. Trading commenced, but the atmosphere seemed tense. A young native (or, a chief, according to some accounts) offered to trade two lemons, one partly eaten, for the Bishop's ring, which the Bishop politely refused. The natives got a little more aggressive, and Epalle thought it would be prudent to head back to the safety of the ship. Father Chaurain, who was a member of the expedition, later gave an account as to what followed,

"We saw the Bishop struck on the head from behind by a native of very short stature, and they set up a horrible war-whoop. The Bishop cried out in pain and put both hands to his head. Now the attack became general, each of the natives selected his own victim. Each of us saw several tomahawks raised over his head, and all ran. (Brother Prosper) saw the Bishop receive another blow from an axe."

Severely wounded, the Bishop was carried back to the ship with most of his clothes and the ring missing. He died three days later and was buried on the uninhabited island of Saint George. Although the missionaries would eventually be allowed back, the mission was not a success. Three missionaries were killed in the couple of years that followed, one died, and the mission was finally abandoned in 1852.

As a Catholic, I have been privileged to work in several Catholic Archives in the capital town of Suva, Fiji. These included the Oceania Marist Province Archives and the Roman Catholic Archives of Fiji. The Marists were the first Catholic missionaries to arrive in Fiji in 1844 in the Lau Group on the eastern edge of the Fiji Archipelago. They had few resources and endured hardships as they evangelized across this group of islands notorious for headhunting and cannibalism. However, just as had been done in the rest of the Pacific, they persevered. Between 1844 and 1941, the Marists had created over thirty mission stations throughout the Fiji islands, most of which are still in use today as parishes. The Marist Archives is small, well organized, and predominantly composed of records written in French.

While volunteering in the archives, I was preserving and processing a photograph collection of the mission stations. Many of the photos were from the late 1800s and contained pictures of churches being built, the land around the churches, and priests and people involved with the missions. The photographs distracted me to a point where I could not look away. They were awkwardly haunting and quite profound. Sitting alone in the two-room archives in what feels like the basement of a house on a dark and rain-drenched day, I was easily transferred into the photo's story as if the mere touch of the photograph were a time machine. One could see an extraordinary change unfolding right before one's very eyes. I could sense the transition that the natives made between their traditional island beliefs and that of Christianity. They were pioneers of the struggle of Christianity but now are only ghosts captured in a photograph album and tucked away in a cabinet. They wait indefinitely for someone else to come along, open up the album, and observe their story.

Today, Christianity has come to dominate spiritual life throughout Melanesia—owing it all to those who laid the groundwork at the end of the eighteenth century and into the nineteenth. Although the missionaries' arrival has caused debate and scornful sentiments for their part in erasing the traditional customs of the islanders, there is no doubt that they immeasurably contributed to the welfare of the islands.

The Marist Archives, Suva, Fiji

The missionaries educated the natives, taught them skills and crafts, brought them medicine, and showed them how to live a healthier life. They brought the islanders law and order way before established governments moved in, and they showed them how to hold their own in the new economic circumstances. All five countries in Melanesia have adopted several different Christian denominations, among them Anglican, Catholic, Wesleyan, Mormon, and Jehovah's Witness. In Fiji, about 65% of the population are Christians, with another 30% Hindu because the Indians who came to these islands as indentured servants decided to stay, and maintained their beliefs. Vanuatu can boast that about 83% of its population is Christian, and most are Presbyterians. The majority of the 85% of Christians in New Caledonia are Catholics. The Solomon Islands is a whopping 92% Christian. This is only upstaged by Papa New Guinea, where 96% of the population cites their religion as Christians. These percentages are certainly impressive. However, as a Catholic and a champion to preserve the traditional way of life, I have mixed feelings about the interference of the missionaries. Fortunately, after traveling extensively in the region for over a decade, I get the sense that the islanders are not ashamed of their traditional beliefs and practices and endeavor to preserve them. This does not mean that women should return to running around topless, but a myriad of customs need to be recaptured, preserved, and passed down to generations.

5

TASTES LIKE PORK

In 1774 an old man named Paowang and a younger one came aboard Captain Cook's ship, the *Resolution*, which was in the bay of the island of Tanna. The two islanders tried the food and drank with the boat's crew. Cook noted that "they gave us to understand in such a manner which admitted of no doubt that they eat human flesh, they began the subject themselves by asking us if we did, otherwise we should never have asked them such a question." Cook, his crew, and the Europeans never imagined before Cook sailed on his first voyage to the region in the late 1760s that Pacific Islanders were cannibals. In fact, Cook and his crew were entirely unprepared for this revelation. When Cook was trying to land two Maori boys in New Zealand, both boys expressed a reluctance to leave the ship. Cook wrote, "They were very unwilling to leave us pretending that they should fall into the hands of their enemies who would kill and eat them." Some of the crew simply thought this was a ploy by the boys to get them back to their own end of the bay. It was not until Cook was in the bay of Ship Cove, New Zealand, that the crew witnessed direct evidence of cannibalism. Joseph Banks, who was a naturalist and botanist and would be a longtime president of the Royal Society in England, was on the *Endeavour* when he witnessed a family preparing food near an earth oven and wrote,

> "Looking carelessly upon one of these we by accident observd 2 bones, pretty clean pick'd, which as appeard upon examination were undoubtedly human bones. Tho we had from the first of our arrival upon the coast constantly heard the Indians acknowledge the custom of eating their enemies we had never before had a proof of it, this amounted almost to demonstration: the bones were clearly human, upon them were evident marks of their having been dressd [i.e. cooked] on the fire, the meat was not intirely pickd off from them and on the grisly ends which were gnawd were evident marks of teeth, and these were accidentaly found in a provision basket. On asking the people what bones were these? they answered, The bones of a man. And have you eat the flesh? – Yes. –Have you none of it left? –No. –Why did you not eat the woman who we saw today in the water? –She was our relation. –Who then is it that you do eat? –Those who are killed in war. –And who was the man whose bones these are? -5 days ago a boat of our enemies came into this bay and of them we killed 7, of whoom the owner of these bones was one."

The reaction to this observation varied among the *Endeavour's* crewmembers. Some were obviously horrified, while others were shocked. Cook, on the other hand, along with Banks, believed that the practice was a custom. Cook wrote, "They eat their enimies Slane in Battell—this seems to come from custom and not from a Savage disposission this they

cannot be charged with—they appear to have but few Vices."
When the people of Europe learned about this practice, they
defined the people of the Pacific Islands as savages. However,
the brutal tradition had a lot more meaning and portraying
the islanders as savages was utterly unjust.

Humans have consecrated the consumption of human
flesh even before the time of modern man. Indeed, Cannibalism, or anthropoid, literally means "man-eating," Paleontolo-
gists have discovered teeth marks on Neanderthal bones that
have had the marrow sucked out. The earliest *Homo sapiens*
bones found in Ethiopia showed signs of de-fleshing by other
humans. Human remains found in Gough's Cave in England,
which dates to about 15,000 B.C., showed evidence of cannibalism by the fact that many of the skulls appeared to have
been used as drinking vessels. As the timeline of humanity
advanced, there has also been evidence of human bones with
kettle polish. This patina develops when bones repeatedly hit
against a metal pot while being cooked. Cannibalism had no
single, ubiquitous meaning but was adapted to suit the spiritual structure of each culture in which it was practiced. Examples of this could be seen in ancient Egypt, where pharaohs
believed that consuming man meant an eternal afterlife, or
the Druids, who believed the act was connected with agriculture and fertility.

Believe it or not, there are five distinct categories of cannibalism. Pathological cannibalism often occurs mainly in serial
killers' behavior where they get some kind of disturbing, grat-
ifying reaction by eating the parts of a human. Autocanni-
balism occurs when a person eats himself, which could be as
innocent as when a person eats his own fingernails to a more
complex and disturbing range of behaviors such as eating the
placenta after giving birth. Both of these types of cannibalism

require psychiatric treatment. The next kind of cannibalism is called learned cannibalistic behavior. This happens in a community of like-minded people who eat someone as a way to terrify others, or steal another's life force to survive starvation conditions. During World War Two in the Pacific theater, Chinese and Japanese soldiers consumed body parts of Prisoners of War. The movie "Alive," where the rugby team that crashed in the Andes Mountains and resorted to eating dead passengers to stay alive, sets a terrific example of survival cannibalism. One often comes across stories of survival cannibalism performed by men lost at sea for weeks. Finally, the last type of cannibalism, which actually resides in a more abstract, spiritual realm, was called symbolic cannibalism. As a Catholic, other Christians and I can, perhaps, relate to this during Mass when I take the wafer and drink the wine that symbolizes the body and blood of Christ.

Cannibalism is considered one of the strongest taboos of all, which could be why it has been recognized as the holiest ritual around the world. This is particularly true in Melanesia. Symbolic and learned cannibalistic behavior were the two types of cannibalism most prevalent throughout the region. Before and during the arrival of the missionaries, the region was rife with cannibalism. Thus the missionaries had a vested interest in stamping out this practice as quickly as possible. However, the tradition was well documented to occur well into the Twentieth Century.

In his book, *Cavorting with Cannibals*, author Rick Williamson wrote that the last priest to be served on the menu was in the early 1960s when a missionary entered a village on Mount Tabwemasana on the island of Espiritu Santos, Vanuatu. Williamson wrote, "a hail of arrows, and swinging nul nuls killed the preacher the moment he set foot in the village. The non-smoking, clean living Christian's untainted meat was cooked in hot stones and enjoyed by everyone, except for those who ate his leathery feet. Some of the naïve cannibals who suffered for aching jaws and indigestion thought his boots were part of the anatomy."

The Melanesians did not kill and eat men for sport. Instead, the practice had a much more profound meaning. Captured enemies from tribal battles were often ritualistically cooked and eaten. In Vanuatu, attackers would carry the corpse of a dead enemy back to their village. They would then cut the body into pieces, sometimes sending an arm or a leg to another friendly village. Men would sing and dance, and the human meat was cooked in a special *laplap*. When consumed, the ingestion was to supposedly absorb *mana* or socio-spiritual power and influence, which enable the consumer to do or get what he wants. Today, the Hua people in Papua New Guinea have a ritual where sons eat the corpse of their fathers and daughters eat those of their mothers. It is believed that this allows the deceased's nu, or vital essence, to be transferred to the next generation.

The missionaries were not the only ones to capture the traditional practice of eating human flesh in their journals, diaries, and reports. Travelers also played a role in reporting their observations. One of these travelers who lived most of her life in Papua New Guinea was author Beatrice Grimshaw. Grimshaw was born in Cloona, Ireland, in 1870, worked as a journalist, an editor for the Irish Cyclist magazine, and became a tour organizer and emigration promoter for an Irish and British steamship company. She would travel around the Pacific Islands between 1903 and 1907, particularly in Melanesia, and would eventually remain in Papua New Guinea from 1907 to 1934. Grimshaw would author thirty-one novels, about eight volumes of short fiction, short stories, dramatic criticism, "dialogues up to date," "telephone talks," career advice to women, and a few non-fiction travelogues. Living in the Victorian age, Grimshaw would experience way more than most women of the time. She left Britain because she needed an emotional and intellectual outlet that she could not have experienced in a world of womanly submission and self-discipline of obligation to class and devotion to religion. Grimshaw was also very aware of violating the standard role model of the early twentieth-century woman and repeatedly addressed this in her books. She was fascinated by gender customs and the role women played in this region, although she was rarely granted any access to women. It was a common practice among the islanders to hide all females at times of danger. This was even noticed and documented by Captain Cook and the missionaries. Nevertheless, in Melanesia, Grimshaw would come across a lot of inexplicable events that would include meeting native magic sorcerers and living in a house that was haunted by ghostly birds.

Grimshaw also had her fair share of encounters with cannibals and headhunters and never shied away from writing about her observations. In the early part of the nineteenth century, cannibalism was still quite prevalent throughout the region. On the island of Malakula in Vanuatu, she came upon a village in the middle of a ceremony. As the heat of the day grew more unbearable by the minute, drums incessantly pounded, men and women danced and chanted. Then, the notorious Chief Atamat emerged from his hut, and everything stopped. He danced a solo dance over about half an acre of ground in pure silence. Grimshaw described the cannibal chief as a man "with a face like an iron devil, and limbs like trunks of trees. Like some evil shadow, he flitted

soundlessly over and over and across the dancing-ground."
Grimshaw was witnessing a cannibal dance used at sacrificial
feasts and believed that all the men in the village had tasted
human flesh. She met an old man who told her that even children got a bone to pick to make them strong. Grimshaw noted
that cannibalism was not an everyday occurrence, and cannibals did not advertise, especially to white people, their affinity
to eat man. If a man got shot in battle, they did not let the
body go to waste, and that revenge often filled the cooking
pots. However, deliberate killing for the sake of eating human
flesh was not common.

When Grimshaw found New Guinea, she knew that she
had found her new home, and adventures would soon follow.
She prided herself on being the first white woman to travel up
the Fly and Sepik rivers of the island country, which she
captured in her 1930 travel book, Isle of Adventure. Along the
way, on these rivers, she would come into contact with headhunters and cannibals. As a resident, she candidly and casu-
ally wrote that most of those who live on the island do not
bother themselves about the cannibals. It was rare to meet
man-eating tribes unless you traveled far into the interior. To
her, the cannibal was not as pictured in fiction—a "howling
savage, whose attitude towards plump and eatable whites like
that of bird towards the worm." She believed that they were
more of a "nervous, timid, over-excitable creature, distrustful
of the strange white race, afraid of it, and anxious to keep out
of its way." Grimshaw heard about a villager from the
Northern coast named Bushimai who escaped from a jail in
Port Moresby with six other prisoners. As they made their way
home through incredible difficulties, the six escapees "never
reached home except vicariously." Bushimai ate them. When
Bushimai was re-captured, a government official (Govamen)

interviewed him, wanting more information about eating human flesh.

Beatrice Grimshaw, Frontispiece of *From Fiji to the Cannibal Islands*

Govamen: "I suppose you found them very tough?"

Bushimai: "I did not find them tough at all."

Govamen: "Well, I can tell you that a friend of mine down the coast was talking to me the other day about that very thing, and he told me that men were always tough."

Bushimai: "Then, I can tell you, with heat, that your friend was not a cook."

Govamen: "No cook?"

Bushimai: "Certainly not. A man is never tough if you cook him right. I grant you. A man will be tough if you cook him carelessly; if you put him in a pot and boil him at a gallop, for instance, but no descent cook ever does such a thing. We bake men... in good stone ovens, built into the side of a hill, with the proper herbs and leaves added. And I can tell you, my chief, that they are not tough then. Far from it."

Bushimai knew that the government official was being biased to this kind of traditional behavior and that the colonial government had tried to put an end to it. But, Bushimai was not shy to talk about cannibalism because he believed that since he was caught and punished, the slate was clean to talk about it.

It is probably a good thing that I do not have much of an anecdote to go along with this chapter. As I sit here on the eve of a controversial election, still in quarantine with over 230,000 Americans dead from the Covid-19 pandemic, my mind and soul wanders to the far away idyllic islands of the Pacific. Physically, I wait in anticipation of the election results, which could have some harmful repercussions in the weeks ahead. I have never really been into politics, but I have never in my life seen a country where the citizens are so divided and so full of hate. For the past four years, the President of the United States has governed like a playground bully, pointing fingers and blaming and name-calling anyone who opposes his beliefs and politics. It has been the most contentious presidency anyone in this country has ever seen. I can remember when my daughter was in grade school, the school (like many schools across the country) took great measures and pains to stamp out "bullying." But the behavior of the President in the past four years has negated all the fine work these schools have implemented.

As I apprehensively wait for a time to be able to travel again, my mind takes me to the beautiful Fijian islands, wondering if I will ever get a chance to return. I have unfinished projects there at the National Archives of Fiji and the Diocese Archives. Both archives are less than a mile apart and are nestled in the middle of the bustling, colonial capital town of Suva. I can recall on one rainy Saturday strolling along the downtown waterway and looking across the bay at the clouds draping over the verdant mountains to the northwest like moss dangling from a tree. It was a wet and quiet day. Not even a cruise ship was in port. Eventually, I sauntered into a cultural market where several stalls sat side-by-side showcasing items from elaborate woodcarvings to cheap tourist trinkets. The owner of the handicrafts operated each stall, and one by one, they each invited me into their booth. Without the cruisers there, I quickly realized that I was the only one there being given the V.I.P. treatment. Fijians are the friendliest, most amicable people on earth. Their smiles are contagious, and their sincerity is beyond reproach. It is hard to believe that they were once feared as the fiercest cannibals on earth. I was never the type of person who could haggle or say no, so I ended up purchasing something from every stall, which put a strain on my budget.

Nevertheless, I can remember looking at some woodcarvings in one of the middle stalls when I picked up a strange, foot-long piece that was ornately decorated with a Fijian design and was in the shape of a squid. The item was skinny and had four prongs at its tip. I held it up high, trying to get a better look in the dim, dank stall. I quizzically looked at the owner, a smiling, enthusiastic man in his fifties, and asked what it was. "A fork," he said. I did not quite understand him from his accent.

"Sorry. A what?" I asked.

"Fork. A traditional fork." I looked at it again. *That's the strangest looking fork I've ever seen,* I thought to myself. I put it back on the table. "A fork for eating people," he added a bit proudly. I swung my head towards him, my interest piqued.

"A cannibal fork?"

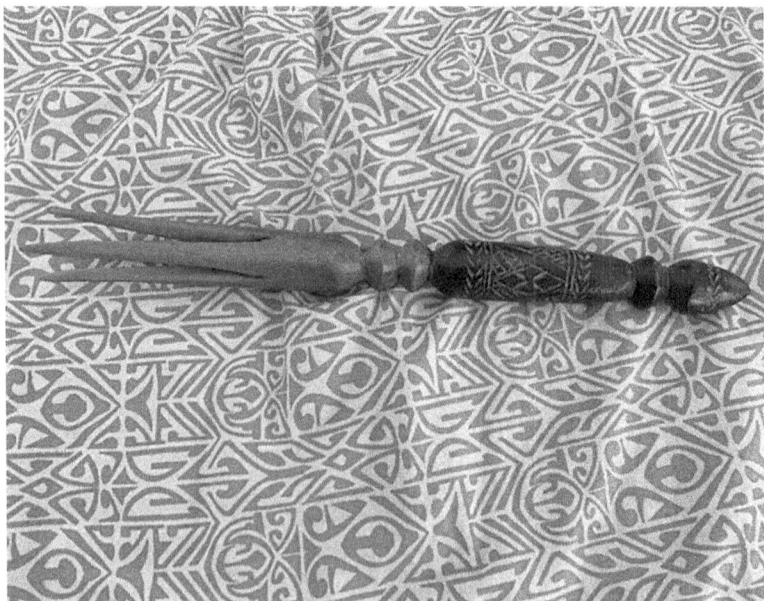

My Fijian Cannibal Fork

"Yes." He said enthusiastically. "Exactly." I looked at it again and bought it. How could I not? At the time, it was kind of a novelty, and when I showed it to family and friends, they were all disgusted by it. But I understood that the fork was part of their historical culture, which they have embraced and can show a sense of humor about it. These days, ornate cannibal forks can be sold in all the tourist shops, as Fijians have publicly embraced their controversial historical and cultural practice.

Fiji had a reputation of being the "cannibal islands" well before the missionaries arrived in the islands. As one may recall, Captain Cook opted to bypass the islands when rumors spread about the natives liking to eat man. Writing about Fiji, he said, "It is said to be populated by Canibals, brave, savage and cruel. That they are Canibals, they themselves do not deny." In 1809 a group of LMS missionaries was stranded on a Fijian island. One of the missionaries, Reverend John Davies, wrote in his diary:

> "The Fejeans are probably the most notable cannibals exist-
> ing. All their islands seem to be divided between petty
> Chiefs who are constantly at war with one another, and
> wherever a man can kill his enemy he will eat him; and
> sometimes hundreds are cut up and baked in ovens at the
> same time, to make a grand feast. They bake the human
> flesh in the same manner the Taheiteans bake their pork."

Cannibalism was regarded as a sacred tradition and was held in reverence by the Fijians of the day. It is believed that the Fijians adopted the practice from their long voyages at sea when the lack of adequate nutrition forced the sailors to consume the dead in order to survive. Once they reached Fiji, cannibalism became part of the native's diet. Because it was regarded as a sacred tradition, the prominent part of dissecting and cooking the meat fell upon the *bete* or priest. Historical evidence has shown that the ceremony of cooking humans took place in pit ovens near the temple, and the chiefs and priests consumed the best choice shares of the meat. One researcher wrote, "the fact that this meat was considered religious and chiefly fare is important as commoners and women only got to eat it in times of particular plenty after a large kill or massacre of enemies and this emphasizes the ancient and religious nature of the custom." Most of the bodies that were eaten were those of enemies taken in battle and were thought of as a way of carrying out harassment, punishment, and humiliation. If the battle was a long way from home, the enemy's bodies were cut up and lightly roasted over an open fire to preserve them before transporting them back to the village. Sometimes, however, if bodies were required for religions or feasting purposes, lower-class people or slaves may be killed or presented as live offerings.

The traditional custom of cannibalism was quite systematic. The meat was scorched over an open fire, and the hair and skin were scrapped off with a kai, or bivalve shell, in the same way pigs are prepared these days. Then, pieces of meat were wrapped in dalo leaves, put in the *lovo* (pit-oven), and baked along with a supply of root crops or even a pig. Many accounts in the region claimed that the meat tasted like pork. Certain utensils, such as forks and pots, were used in the feast, and special chants and drumbeats were composed for the occasion. People of lower rank and women generally did not partake in the feast, except for women of higher rank who would have secretly eaten human flesh, especially if large quantities were available. Besides human flesh, the other parts of the body were used for functional purposes. For example, teeth were needed for necklaces or were inlaid on war clubs. Skulls were made into soup or kava bowls for the chiefs and priests, and bones were used canoe sail needles.

Headhunting, which seemed synonymous with cannibalism, was actually its own traditional ritual and practiced throughout Melanesia, particularly in Papua New Guinea and the Solomon Islands. It was related to achieving and maintaining power and authority, and chiefs acquired skulls like trophies. The skull was believed to contain a *mana*-like force, and the practice was entrenched in native tradition going back to prehistoric times. For example, in many Melanesian islands such as Roviana, Solomon Islands chiefs and warriors used headhunting for their own political legitimacy. An accumulation of skulls was a highly visible display of their status. Raids were never executed until villagers received approval from the spiritual world through a ritual specialist who often reached out to the ancestors for protection. By taking the head back to one's own village, warriors could incorporate the enemy's spirit into their own community. Villagers might even give the head a new name or treat it with respect as a way to persuade the spirit to join the community. The heads were also needed for the inauguration of a new communal house or a new war canoe to ensure the canoe's warring success. Thus, headhunting was a tool of political intimidation entangled with a complex view of the world and its spiritual dominance over human life and actions.

With the advent of missionaries and colonial governments, the end of headhunting came fairly quickly by the early 1900s. As late as 1923, the traveler Beatrice Grimshaw was reporting her headhunting encounters while traveling the Sepik River in Papua New Guinea. Heads were everywhere.

She wrote, "Every village had a display of heads in its men's communal house; every canoe that came about the launch offered a head." She was impressed how every person who came to her launch had a story about headhunting raids of "yesterday and last week." When Grimshaw visited Lake Murray, she noted that headhunting was the main activity and the only excitement in the area. She also witnessed the importance of the possession of heads, the preparation and painting of their specimens, and the proper display of the finished work. "They can sever a protesting, fighting head as ably as a butcher can cut the throat of a sheep, although the knives of shell or bamboo generally used by them are very unsatisfactory tools." Upon the Fly River, Grimshaw fascinatedly reported how the village "taxidermist" prepared the trophy head:

> "He opens the scalp at the back, removes the bones of the head, and smokes and cures the skin converting it into a thick soft leather. This he stuffs out into an extraordinary shape, half human, half animal, lacing up the split at the back and the base of the neck with strips of cured skin that are exactly like porpoise-hide bootlaces. After stuffing, it is painted all over black, ornamented with white an red; the nose is elevated by means of a piece of bamboo, and the open mouth filled with white stones to represent teeth. Long locks of fibre, representing hair, are fastened on; sometimes feathers are added."

One cannot deny the clever and artistic merit in this work. Grimshaw understood that the heads were treated as special treasures, but she also was surprised that the heads were not above being sold. She jested, "one four-shilling knife, one head, was the standard price, and we could probably have bought every available head, alive or dead."

On November 13, 2003, villagers from the remote Nabu-tautau Village located in the headwaters of the Sigatoka River on Fiji's main island of Viti Levu formally apologized to descendants of a British missionary, Reverend Thomas Baker, who had been killed and eaten. Approximately eleven descendants attended the ceremony and were accompanied by Prime Minister Laisenia Qarase and about six hundred islanders. The ritual of reconciliation was also designed to lift a curse under which the local inhabitants believed they had been suffering since the murder. During the ceremony, one spokesman said, "The tears were from our hearts deep inside because we have waited for so long for this moment. Today we will be set free from the curse." The ceremony included the traditional drinking of kava and a symbolic cutting the chain of the curse and bondage over the village. The chief at the time, who was Ratu Filimoni Nawawabalevu, said, "We believe we must have been cursed, and we must apologize for what happened... when we have made the apology we will be clean again."

In 1865 The Reverend Thomas Baker, a Methodist missionary, was appointed as the "Missionary of the Interior" of Fiji and made long journeys into the interior of Viti Levu. The villages in this part of the island were untouched by Christian influences. In July of 1867, the Rev. Baker and seven converted Fijian Christian teachers arrived in Nabuatautau village and were coldly received by Chief Nawawabalavu. The group was unaware that a chief from a nearby hostile village had offered Nawawabalavu a *tabua* (whale tooth), which could only be obtained by beached whales or by trades, making them highly rare, sacred, and coveted. The *tabua* offering was a request to kill Baker, who had visited the hostile village earlier. The legend goes that Baker had left his comb lying on a mat in the chief's hut. Because all property in the village was for communal use, the chief had no inhibitions in picking it up and putting it in his hair. Irritated that the chief was using his comb Baker snatched it back, touching the chief's head. This sealed his fate, as the head of a chief was considered the area where his power dwelled and was sacred. As Baker and his group were leaving the village the next morning, they were ambushed, clubbed, decapitated, and eventually eaten. Only two of Baker's men made it out alive and reported the grim event to the Mission authorities. The author, Jack London, heard about this incident and wrote a short story titled "The Whale Tooth." The story was published in 1909 and was about an unfortunate innocent man's death because of a culture clash where two men were incapable of mutual understanding. Rev. Baker would be the last European killed and eaten in Fiji.

Although natives from the Melanesian region were known for their voracious appetite for human flesh, particularly in the nineteenth century, there were two chiefs from the Fiji Islands whose renowned reputations as insatiable cannibals have dubbed them the "King of the Cannibals." The first was chief Udre Udre from a village near Rakiraki in the northern area of the island of Viti Levu. His birth and death are unrecorded, but scholars believe he died circa 1840. In 1849, a missionary named Richard Lyth was taken to the chief's tomb and made a gruesome observation. He found a long row of 872 stones with many gaps where some stones had been removed. Each stone represented a person that Udre Udre ate. Lyth wrote, "Ravatu, a son of the above prince of cannibals took me out of the town about a mile to show me the stones by which his father memorialised the number of human beings that he ate from time to time beginning after his family had begun to grow up until the beginning of turning a little gray." Ravutu assured the missionary that his father killed his victims in war and ate them all. He gave none to nobody. Ravutu also told Lyth that his father ate nothing else but human flesh, and what he could not eat in one sitting he would keep preserved in a box. According to documented accounts, the number of people Udre Udre ate was between 872 and 999 and earned him the honor of being named Guinness World Records *Most Prolific Cannibal.*

The second famous cannibal of Fiji was chief Seru Epenisa Cakobau, who was already mentioned as the ruler of the Kingdom of Fiji from 1871 to 1874 before being forced to ask for British annexation of the islands. Cakobau was a proud cannibal before converting himself to Christianity and renouncing cannibalism. Nevertheless, Cakobau loved playing a cat and mouse game with the missionaries before becoming a Christian. He wanted to squeeze every advantage he could out of the missionaries before taking a step for *lotu* (entering the church). One missionary who visited Fiji in 1847 wrote, "I received a visit from Cakobau... He is an absolute ruler: whom he will he kills, and whom he will he keeps alive. Upon the whole, he is rather favourable to our mission here, but does not *lotu*. He professes great dislike to the introduction of Popery. War is his delight, and feasting on the bodies of the slain..." Cakobau either rejected the missionaries or, when it was beneficial to him, enticed them with the prospect of his eventual conversion. He knew that conversion was on the horizon, and he saw that many of the other Fijian chiefs were converting because of the advantages of having Christians on their side. But Cakobau remained wily about politics and converting to Christianity. A fascinating yet ironic conversation was captured between Reverend John Hunt and Chief Cakobau:

Chief Cakobau: "If I am the first to become a Christian among my people, I shall be first in heaven, shall I not?"

The Missionary: "If you love God the most, and serve Him the best, you may have a higher place in heaven."

Chief Cakobau: "But chief Namosimalua has become a Christian. Have you given him glass windows for his new house, and English carpets for his floors, and have you sent to England for a vessel for him? He gets no riches because he has renounced heathenism."

RATU SERU CAKOBAU

Chief Ratu Cakobau of Fiji. Photo from National Archives of Fiji

The Missionary: "We do not come here to give riches to those who become Christians, but to tell you about God and Jesus Christ, that you may love Him, and your souls be saved."

Chief Cakobau: "Then I will not become a Christian. What will become of the bodies of those who have been eaten, and those who have been buried? Will they rise again from the dead?"

The Missionary: "Your body, the bodies of all those whom you have eaten, and the bodies of all who are in the graves, will rise again at the day of judgment; and if you and they have not repented, you will all be condemned and cast into hell-fire."

Chief Cakobau: "Ah, well! It is a fine thing to have a fire in cold weather."

The cannibal king finally declared himself a convert on April 30, 1854. Having become a Christian, Cakobau would pardon all the captives on the battlefield instead of using the traditional practice of humiliating, killing, and eating the defeated men. Although the practice of eating human flesh would soon fade, the stories continue to be told in the bizarre corners of the island, as well as they suddenly emerge from the darkest shadows of the region. One just has to make that effort to look for them.

6

NEVER TRUST A SINGING VELE BIRD

As a collector of Pacific Islands' legends, there is one from Papua New Guinea that I have always enjoyed. The story not only teaches us how bats became to be on the island, but it also contains a theme of the empowerment of women, which one does not see very often in stories from this particularly patriarchal part of the world. Even more profoundly, there is a hint that the women in this legend use sorcery to teach the men of the village a lesson. The legend is titled, The Bat Women of Koitabu:

> In the old days, the men of the tribal group of Koitabu were great hunters, and the women worked hard in the gardens. In the afternoons, when they returned from hunting and gardening, these people would make feasts, and in the evenings they would sit by the fire, chewing betel-nut, talking and telling stories. They were happy until a time came when the men of the tribe stopped bringing home meat. They had become lazy and greedy; they hunted only

enough meat for themselves, and ate it as soon as they caught it.

The women, as usual, went on bringing their bags of produce from the gardens. They were puzzled and disappointed when the men returned empty-handed from the bush each day. The hunters no longer brought back meat and told the women they had not been able to catch anything. So the women and children ate only the vegetables and fruit from the gardens in the evening and they grew thin and felt hungry. But the men were as strong and looked as well-nourished as ever.

Among the hunters was one young tribesman, Gaigo, who was newly married to a woman called Au. Gaigo loved Au and he was worried to see her growing thin. When the hunters devoured their meat in the bush, he would hide a morsel in his hair and take it home to Au. He told her she must keep this a secret between them.

One day, the women had become suspicious of their husbands. "I do not think the men are telling the truth when they say they cannot find any meat, the chief's wife declared. "Why should we toil in the gardens and bring home our food for such lazy, greedy men to share?"

Then Au spoke up, "My husband is a good man, he brings me home pieces of meat. It is true that the men still find meat in the bush. They hunt only enough for themselves, and eat it before they come home."

The other women muttered angrily when they heard this. "Why should we be cheated this way?"

"We will not go to the gardens today," the chief's wife said. "Instead, we will go into the bush and look for black feathers. We must all bring back as many feathers as we can find." So the women did this.

That day, both the men and women returned home empty handed. The men complained bitterly when they saw there were no vegetables or fruit for them to eat. "You lazy women!" scolded the chief. "What have you been doing all day?"

The next day the women went to the banana garden, where the chief's wife showed them how to sew together all the black feathers they had collected. When they had finished doing this, each woman tied the sewn feathers to her arms. Then the chief's wife stepped forward and said, "Tireless women of Koitabu! Our selfish husbands have deceived us for too long! Let us live our own lives, and leave them at home. Let the men look after our children in future! Come with me- we will go into the forest and find our men and bid them goodbye, and then we will fly away forever."

There was a loud noise as all the women save one flapped their black wings, and then they took to the air in a huge flock. Only Au did not join the others; she stayed behind, faithful to the young husband who had proved his love for her.

The bat-women flew over the treetops and found the men feasting on wild pigs. The women circled above them and their husbands looked up fearfully. They were amazed when they recognized the strange creatures above them as their wives. "You! You have deceived us all these days!" the women cried. "We are leaving you forever. Go back to the village. The children are waiting for you!"

As they spoke, the women flitted from branch to branch of a tall tree. "In future you will never see us during the day, but you may see us after sunset when we fly about in the cool darkness." These were the last words the women spoke to their husbands. Rustling their black wings, they flew off and spread to different hiding places.

"The Bat Women of Koitabu," illustration by Tara Bonvillain

The men ran back to their homes and cried pitifully, mourning as though someone had died. And there they found Au, the only wife left in the village telling the children how their mothers had turned themselves into bats and flown away.

Ever since that time, bats have lived in dark, secret places. They come out when darkness falls- but you will never see them flying about during the day.

The belief in sorcery, or witchcraft, throughout the Melanesian region has been accepted as a cultural practice and carries significant weight in most aspects of public and private lives. The Papua New Guinea's Sorcery Act of 1971 puts magic and witchcraft together under the umbrella of sorcery, stating, "Sorcerers have extraordinary powers that can be used sometimes for good purposes, but more often for bad ones." The anthropologist E.E. Evans-Pritchard, perhaps, defined sorcery and witchcraft a little better. "Sorcery refers to the deliberate use of magical rituals to injure, kill, or cause misfortune, and witchcraft refers to an unconscious capacity to harm others." During colonial times, missionaries tried to distinguish magic as being benevolent and aimed at improving life, while sorcery was more malevolent designed to cause harm. Speculation of the use of sorcery especially rises when the victim was an important person or leader, was in his or her prime, or if the death was sudden or unexpected. However, deaths of the very elderly were not considered a result of sorcery. Interestingly, when reviewing police reports, the cases of sorcery have shown victims who have been buried alive, beheaded, pushed from high cliffs, electrocuted, forced to drink petroleum, stoned to death, or shot.

Sorcery involves calculated and deliberate actions by a person who intends to harm others, which is done through ritual means or incantations. In Melanesia, many sorcery techniques are acquired from relatives or friends and passed down from generation to generation. The most common approach is personal leavings sorcery, which involves the sorcerer manipulating the victim's personal features such as hair, fingernails, or an item that the victim has used or touched. After creating a spell, the sorcerer will wrap the leavings in a parcel and dispose of them in a manner according to the desired effect. Another approach is assault sorcery, which happens when the sorcerer uses magic that makes the victim unconscious. They then insert objects such as needles into the body or would remove internal organs.

Projectile sorcery occurs when the sorcerer magically shoots things, such as pieces of glass or wire, into the victim's body. Another powerful technique of sorcery involves the use of spirits of either the dead or the living to attack the victim. Some sorcerers use poisons or other toxic substances that are either put on the tips of arrows during battles or added to food, water, or other things that are consumed.

Author, Rick Williamson, described how human bones were the key ingredients that a ni-Vanuatu sorcerer used to kill victims in his book, *Cavorting with Cannibals.* The bones were ground into a white powder, and "depending on what type of tabu leaf is milked into the residue" was used to kill. Sometimes the bones were burnt to black ash and used to evoke spirits during displays of magic. "Powder that's made from the bones of different body parts was used to kill in various ways. Some powders were used to poison food and others were blown from the palm of the hand and carried by the wind to render a victim weak and helpless before they are physically killed." Indeed, sorcerers have to be very cautious and only blow white powder into the wind. They know better than to blow black powder into the wind because if it flows back into their face the result could mean death to the sorcerer himself.

Today, the use of sorcery and black magic are very prevalent in certain parts of Melanesia, and as one high profile parliamentarian in Papua New Guinea said, "We respect the law and Christian ethics, but the beliefs in sorcery are a way of life." It is interesting to note that the missionaries successfully eradicated some of the aspects of cultural life in Melanesian, such as cannibalism, infanticide, and widow strangling, but they did not eliminate sorcery or black magic. Perhaps, this is because they believe that supernatural forces could influence the course of events in the physical world. For example, the missionaries did not have to believe that evil spirits caused sickness. Yet, they acknowledged that it was sent by God and encouraged prayer as a supernatural way of healing. The biblical culture of the first century CE was very similar to the Melanesian culture encountered by the missionaries, especially with the issue that spirits and magic can cause sickness. Pastors and priests throughout the region emphasize the power of prayer and faith in Jesus Christ to defeat the power of black magic and evil spirits. Therefore, it would be hypocritical for the missionaries and the clergymen of today to denounce sorcery. Good conquers evil. Good Christians do not need to fear the power of sorcery when prayer and faith in God will protect one from human and spiritual enemies.

One of the main issues, however, is the growing problem of men and women being accused of witchcraft or sorcery that leads to being physically, emotionally, and sexually tortured, and then left severely wounded or even often killed. Accusations of sorcery usually happen because of several factors that include jealousy due to social and economic advancement, customary land disputes between different clans and tribes, criminal activities within the village, and friendship breakdowns. Sometimes an accused sorcerer who survives the incriminating evidence will face lifetime banishment along with their family from the community. Witch-hunts arise, and communities practically become hostages, usually by a group of "boys" as an assertion of power. Still, more often than not, many people contribute to the violence, such as those who physically carry it out, those who lead or direct it, and those who encourage and support it. There is also a spectrum of motivations that accusers use to attack alleged sorcerers. These range from having genuine fear, to a misplaced desire to fix injustice, to personal motivations like financial gain or a chance to be a hero or settling a past score. Regardless, there is no doubt that violence against alleged sorcerers has become a human rights issue. Indeed, the action taking against sorcerers, particularly concerning women, has attracted Human Rights Defenders who will try to intervene when possible to provide critical support such as administering medical treatment or counseling.

Living in the Western world, it is difficult to believe in the supernatural. Many media sources spend a lot of time trying to prove the existence of the supernatural. But, whom are we kidding? It is mainly to raise media viewership and line people's pockets with cash. In Melanesia, however, there is a genuine belief that something good or evil could happen metaphysically. During my travels in the region, I tried to avoid controversial topics with colleagues and friends, reminding myself that I am a volunteer and not some rabble-rouser. But every so often, I just have to ask questions whenever something unusual shows itself or comes to mind.

One day I decided to ask Bishop Terry Brown if he ever had any experience dealing with sorcery during his career in the Solomon Islands. I thought for sure that since he was a clergyman from the West, he would scoff at the question. But he did not. He told me that in the late 1970s when he was teaching at Kohimarama on the island of Guadalcanal (about 24 miles from Honiara), a student from the Malaita Island brought in his brother from town who had been poisoned by *arua* sorcery. Bishop Terry said, "He writhed on the floor of my

living room like a snake." The student explained that the
sorcery method was feeding some of his brother's food to a
snake with a magic spell. Thus he was now behaving like a
snake. The Bishop prayed with the student, which seemed to
have little effect on the wiggly brother, and the boys' family
also tried using custom medicine to no avail. Finally, the next
night the Warden from town performed a full-scale exorcism
that seemed to help. My jaw dropped to the floor like a
cartoon character. I was not expecting to hear such a story
from Bishop Terry. I wondered and asked myself *what other
adventures did he endure during his tenure in the region.* He then
told me to Google *arua* sorcery in Malaita for more explana-
tions and to get a better understanding.

Two kinds of sorcery are practiced in the Solomon Islands.
Arua is a kind of sorcery practiced mostly in Malaita in which
a male or female takes food scraps or a piece of clothing of
another person and feeds it to a snake, frog, or rat. *Vele* is
mainly practiced on the island of Guadalcanal, and the usual
method is for a sorcerer to hide by the side of the road and
make sharp noises to attract the attention of his victim as he
or she approaches. The victim will see the sorcerer's *vasa* (usually a small bag where the magical power of vele resides and
contains items such as sacred earth, pieces of shrub, a man's
tooth, and native shell money) suspended from a finger. The
word *"vele"* means to pinch from the tingling or pinched
feeling in the arms that warns protected persons of the proximity of the *vele* sorcerer. Upon seeing this, the victim will
become unconscious and collapse. There is a perception that
it is difficult to prove these types of sorcerers in court,
primarily because they practice their magic in secret or hide
their magical articles. Indeed, they can be caught. For example, a sorcerer who practices *aura* often dances in the grave-

yard after their victim is buried. A *veleI* sorcerer can be caught in possession of the *vele* bag, which is known within the courts as containing items for harmful magic.

Bishop Terry came across a similar incident as the one just recently told with his predecessor, Bishop Raymond Aumae, who was the Bishop of Malaita from 1990 to 1994. Bishop Raymond believed that he could discern *arua* and who the sorcerer was. Once the sorcerer was determined, people would go to him or her, accuse him or her, ask that the spell be removed, and ask for compensation. In one case, Bishop Raymond made an accusation, which proved to be false. The accused sorcerer demanded compensation from Bishop Raymond, which he ultimately paid. Bishop Terry, on the other hand, discouraged the process of trying to discern who was the sorcerer and instead suggested that people simply seek healing for the person who was the victim. As a westerner in these matters, Bishop Terry was more inclined to regard the whole process as mere superstition rather than reality. But he understood that the natives regarded the practice of sorcery as a tangible phenomenon.

On Guadalcanal, Bishop Terry listened to many stories dealing with sorcery, and he also had to fulfill strange requests occasionally. One of the most common stories was how islanders became terrified at night whenever they heard the *vele* bird that accompanies the sorcerer with his little sack of magic tied around his neck. The vele man would hold his little sack in front of the victim, who then drops dead of fright. He would then quickly disappear. Other unusual experiences that Bishop Terry became involved with mainly dealt with removing curses placed on people and places, which one time included an entire village. Bishop Terry chuckled, "It's all part of the job in Melanesia." He even once removed a curse from a village soccer team who believed that they were jinxed by a priest who did not feel that he was fed well enough during his stay in the village. I was thinking, *Man, where were you over the years for all the cursed soccer teams I played for?*

Even Bishop Terry agreed that the greatest danger was that the belief in sorcery led to criminal activities against those accused of performing the practice. For example, in 2009, a pagan priest in East Kwaio, Malaita Province, was suspected of practicing sorcery and was stabbed to death. In 2010 relatives of a dead man burnt down two homes in separate villages in Central Kwara'ae, Malaita Province, because they suspected their relative had died due to sorcery. Additionally, some of the customary healers or doctors would sometimes take advantage of the strong beliefs in sorcery to commit sexual offenses towards female victims of sorcery-belief sickness like rape and indecent assault. Lately, the Law Reform Commission has urged the public not to assault any person suspected of sorcery but instead encouraged them to file reports to the police with evidence. In the Solomon Islands, sorcery was an offense under Penal Code [Cap 26] in Section 190, which addresses sorcery offenses, but it must be proven in court. The issue was that people took the law into their own hands without reporting such matters to the police. Also, the Penal Code had two problems. It did not reflect sorcery as it was known and understood in society, and it was difficult to prove in court because its conduct and dealings were usually done in secret.

I have found over the years that the Pacific Islands is a great place to run and hide. Most American tourists stop in Hawaii. But if they only traveled a little more south, they would find that they could have an entire beach to themselves. For me, the islands, especially Melanesia, seemed isolated, idyllic, and an incredibly unique place to invigorate a passion, which for me was helping to preserve the memory of these island nations. In fact, the motto at the National Archives of Solomon Islands is "*Haus Blong Memori*" (house of memories), which I absolutely love. This is partially how my nonprofit organization, Island Culture Archival Support, came to be. In fact, it is how most nonprofits begin—with a passion. I knew that I was not going to get rich with this idea. However, living in a country where you are judged by who and what you are, or what kind of car you drive, it was nice to escape to a place where I was not required to answer these questions. Perhaps, this American character trait is what is driving the Covid-19 pandemic death toll in the U.S. People will not stay home because they egotistically and narcissistically believed that what they do is too important, and they have to continue showing "who" they are. At the time of this paragraph, the death toll was pushing 30,000 people. I preferred to travel to Pacific Islands, especially Melanesia, where the islanders seemed to sincerely accept me for "how" I am, especially within the environment. This is a little deeper and more difficult. If anything, Melanesia has taught me that it is a great place to spend some time soul searching.

My first (and actually my one and only) sorcery encounter occurred one day while working at the National Archives of the Solomon Islands. The belief that sorcerers have used supernatural powers to harm other people is a common view, and most people do not accept natural causes in case of illness or the death of relatives and friends. On this occasion, in September of 2010, I had stopped at the National Archives to say goodbye to the staff before making the long journey home. My colleague, Kabini, the Archives' conservator at the time, hesitantly approached me and apologized for not being around to do something with me over the weekend. He did not have to be so apologetic as I was capable of entertaining myself. I knew something was not quite right with him, though. Kabini was an affable young man with a heart-warming smile and was always in a good mood. "My aunt passed away on Friday," he continued with teary eyes. "I had to attend family get-togethers."

"No worries," I replied. "I'm sorry to hear this." Kabini avoided eye contact with me. I could tell that there was more he wanted to tell me. I reached down to fuss with one of my bags, hoping to ease the moment.

"We think she was killed by a sorcerer," he finally proclaimed. I immediately stopped what I was doing and looked up at him. I can see the anger and frustration on his face.

"Really?" I did not know what to say. This was the first I had ever heard about an actual sorcery event. To me it was just a topic in books and movies. Kabini's aunt was only in her forties and had recently taken a higher position in one of the Government Ministries. He suspected jealousy as the reason the black magic was cast upon her. Although I was immediately intrigued, I did not want to blurt out a cultural *faux pas* which I was so apt to do. Naturally, I had a million questions I wanted to ask. I played it safe and simply asked if he knew who the sorcerer was. Kabini shook his head.

"No. It's difficult. But with the help of a priest, we might be able to track the magic to the creator." I wished him the best of luck and left it at that. My plane was beckoning me. But, I had to admit that Kabini's story kind of spooked me. As I was driven to the airport late that afternoon, I remember staring at the neighborhoods and looking beyond the small, tin-roofed houses. Every fourth house seemed to have a pile of debris or trash burning in the yard, and the white and black smoke mixed with the shadows of the jungle. It was surreal and ominous looking. I could hear the music theme from the movie, *The Exorcist*, ringing throughout my head. The imagery made me ask myself, *what actually goes on in the dark neighborhoods of the jungle?* To me, the shadows on these beautiful Melanesian islands were not all picturesque and peaceful as the tourism brochures made them look to be and often had a more sinister story to tell.

For the next decade, I would sporadically come across fascinating articles regarding the use of sorcery throughout Melanesia and would collect them with a ghastly curiosity. Except for New Caledonia, the practice seemed to grow into bigger issues involving local courts, governments, and churches all over Melanesia. For example, I found a news release from 2005 about sorcery cases in Fiji. One of them was about how villagers burned artifacts as part of a spiritual cleansing process by torching the items used for witchcraft. A team was lead by a reverend from the Methodist church helped islanders from several villages on the island of Viti Levu identify dark items and set them ablaze. The team had to be invited into the village, but they found that their hindrance for spiritual growth was from the fear of superstitious beliefs and witchcraft. More recently, in 2020, a Fijian chief, Ratu Makutu Nagagavoka, pleaded with his villagers to stop the practice of witchcraft in the province and called on his people to worship God instead.

In 2014, a horrible incident on an island near Malekula, Vanuatu, occurred that involved a community including chiefs and church pastors who hung two men on suspicion of using sorcery. After the incident, a high-ranking parliament member took a stand against sorcerers he blamed were at fault with the brutal retaliation from the community. The parliament member felt that the use of sorcery should be considered an extreme crime, and people who practiced it should get the death penalty. He noted the frustration in the difficulties of finding evidence beyond all reasonable doubt to punish those using black magic. In fact, only a small percentage of alleged sorcerers were ever brought to justice. It was more of an acknowledgment that sorcery, indeed, exists deep within the customs of the people without any regard to the potential backlash from governmental authorities or that of the international community. The parliament member noted, "The international community, they do not have the same tradition as us. Our constitution says Vanuatu is founded on Melanesian traditional values and then followed by Christian principles. So our traditional Melanesian values do exist, the good and bad sides of it."

The Vanuatu island of Ambrym has long been considered a hotbed of black magic, and the islanders are feared as very powerful *nakaimas* (sorcerers). For example, in Port Vila, a student from a school accidentally drowned, and the people started to question the school's principal simply because he was from Ambrym. The principal subsequently resigned rather than face more harassment. As author Rick Williamson delved deeper into the world of I in Vanuatu, he shared his bizarre experiences with Ambrym sorcerers while visiting the island. Before he left for the island, he told his ni-Vanutau friend of his plans of visiting Ambrym and noted that the muscles in his friend's smiling face contorted to a frown of concern. The friend warned him that he was about to enter the "heart of a demonic beast" and that just mentioning the island could send shockwaves of fear through superstitious villagers. Despite the warnings, Williamson went anyway and documented his every encounter with the supernatural.

On Ambrym, Williamson met a *nakaima* named Joe who tried to show him a few examples of magic, but Williamson dismissed them as clever tricks and wanted to experience something more concrete. He stated that he wanted to "feel the raging energy of supernatural spirit firsthand." While Williamson waited at the edge of a *natsaro* (dance ground), Joe then disappeared into the forest and returned ten minutes later, chewing a cud of dark green leaves and carrying a sturdy sapling and a *namele* leaf into the center of the *natsaro*. He then drove the stick into the soft ground and created a hole about seven inches deep, and placed the stem of the leaf into the hole. Joe then spat his mouthful of leaves into the hole and gently tampered around the base of the *namele* six times.

Once Joe's preparation was complete, it was time to unleash the sorcerer's power. Before any magic was to take place, Williamson made sure not to make any eye contact with Joe or any other sorcerer in the proximity of the *natsaro* for fear of being hypnotized. Then, Joe picked a young and powerfully built villager and challenged him to pull the leaf from the ground. The villager huffed and puffed, but no matter how hard he tried, he could not pull the leaf from the ground. Williamson raised an eyebrow, but still, the villager could have been acting. Joe then called for Williamson to give it a go. Williamson walked up to the leaf and used every muscle he had but could not budge the leaf. Williamson wrote, "When I couldn't shift the leaf, this went way beyond the sphere of anything I'd ever experienced. This was an intimate liaison with the supernatural." However, Williamson was not about to give up. "By channeling every ounce of my energy, and with dogged determination, I slowly started to pull the leaf from the ground." Then, something incredible happened. As Williamson was successfully pulling the leaf, "An unfathomable force reached up from the bowels of the earth, and with a violent jerk, it wrenched the leaf back into the soft soil." This moment of experiencing a sudden surge of supernatural power was quite frightening and "went way beyond an honest person unwittingly deceiving himself or being deceived by having some hidden vortex in his subconscious manipulated." Williamson then graciously thanked the sorcerers, grabbed his packs, and went straight to the airport in Woru, where he caught the next available flight off the island.

While working at the Vanuatu National Library and Archives and spending a fair amount of time in the country, I had no inkling that sorcery was being practiced and was completely naïve of the topic. Naivety keeps the soul innocent. But once I had my little encounter with Kabini in Honiara, I started to examine and question my Melanesian environment more closely. I noticed that sorcery was not discussed in public but is quite endemic. When people died suddenly, there was often community gossip relating to black magic. Vanuatu, for example, is officially a Christian country with the motto, "*Long God yumi stanap* (in front of God we stand)," so people do not usually come forth and openly say that they believe in sorcery. But the undercurrent belief and practice of sorcery still lies within the communities under the surface of everyday life.

Of all the Melanesian countries, it is Papua New Guinea that has experienced the most problems with the belief in sorcery to a point where it has been spiraling out of control. Sorcery was an ancient practice that had played an integral role in the lives of the islanders and had roots in the traditional Melanesian preoccupation with the workings of spirits. Indeed, the practice was once used in traditional healing, to improve crops, and in times of war.

The Vanuatu National Archives

Papua New Guinea has some 800 languages, and in recent years many of these various ethnic groups began migrating to other parts of the country, mixing cultures. Over the last several decades, this rapid cultural change has caused great disruption for many Papua New Guineans, who sometimes resort to corrupted cultural norms. As they try to maneuver through this confusion of change, blame for when bad things happen resulted in a significant increase in attacks and killings. Sister Lorena Jenal, a Swiss nun who has lived in Papua New Guinea for more than thirty years, recently gained recognition for her efforts to help the victims of sorcery-related attacks. She believes that the reliance on sorcery is a result of confusion in people's lives. To Sister Jenal, the people of Papua New Guinea have been thrown together from the Stone Age into a very technical, computerized world, and it has gone too fast for them. She also noted that the Covid-19 pandemic has left people confused, leading to a rise in cases where the victims are accused of practicing sorcery.

This is not far from one of the reasons that drove the infamous Salem witch trials in the Massachusetts Bay Colony of America. For those colonists, the eyes of the world were watching them try to succeed in a new environment. When something went wrong such as crop losses, disease epidemics, or political strife, it was easy to blame your neighbor for the failure. But that was the late seventeenth century. This is modern-day Papua New Guinea. From 1996-2016 analysis of newspaper records and court filings led by the Papua New Guinea National Research Institute and compiled by the Australian National University found that there were on average of thirty killings a year from attacks on those accused of sorcery. Some governments put an even higher estimate at a bewildering 500 deaths a year. Recently the governor of the Oro province told the Papua New Guinea newspaper that the persistent sorcery-related violence is a "red flag" that the country is regressing in its attempts to deal with the problem. He added, "Sorcery related violence stems from poor education, lack of awareness, limited opportunities coupled with deteriorating capacity for law and order and a lack of political will." In 2013 the Sorcery Act of 1971, which mandated that all killings related to sorcery accusations would be treated as murder, was repealed after photographs spread through social media of a 20-year old woman from the highlands city of Mount Hagen who was murdered. She was stripped, doused in gasoline, and burned to death after being accused of witch-craft following the death of a local boy. Amazingly, from the inception of the Sorcery Act, no perpetrator of an alleged sorcery-related killing had ever been convicted of murder.

Some of the earliest written sorcery experiences in Papua New Guinea have come from travelers in the early part of the twentieth century. One of these travelers was Caroline Mytinger, a twenty-nine-year-old woman from Cleveland, Ohio, who modeled as a "Gibson Girl" for the famous illustrator Charles Dana Gibson. She was also a talented artist with a passion for travel. In 1926 Mytinger, with her long-time friend Margaret Warner, sailed from San Francisco to Melanesia. As they sailed through the Golden Gate Bridge on a foggy March day, Mytinger recalled that they were unencumbered "by the usual equipment of expe-ditions: by endowment funds, by precedents, doubts, supplies, an expedition yacht or airplane, by even the bless-ings or belief of our friends and families, who said we couldn't do it." For three years the pair trounced about the Solomon Islands and Papua New Guinea where Mytinger wanted to realize her dream of capturing "vanishing primi-tives" with paints and brushes. Before the women returned to the United States in 1929, she had produced a copious number of oil portraits, sketches, and photographs. The paintings were exhibited in the 1930s at the New York City's American Museum of Natural History, the Brooklyn Museum, and other museums around the country. One of Mytinger's favorite models was a headhunter named Taupa-raupi, who was brought to her as part of a group taken pris-oner by the authorities for allegedly beheading and eating thirty-nine people of a neighboring village. In 1942, about the time the United States was fighting the Japanese on

Guadalcanal, she published a book titled, *Headhunting in the Solomon Islands: Around the Coral Sea*. Letters that she wrote to her family and friends during her adventure formed the basis of this book, and it spent several weeks on the *New York Times* bestseller list. Her second book, *New Guinea Headhunt*, published in 1946, featured Tauparaupi's portrait on the front cover.

Although Mytinger and Warner witnessed very strange events throughout their trip, one of the strangest experiences happened near Rabaul, Papua New Guinea, where a sorcerer became infatuated with a young, married woman who lived in the same village. The woman told the sorcerer that she wanted nothing to do with him, but he persisted and warned her that he would put a love spell on her. This kind of threat usually worked because villagers knew that if a woman had a spell placed on her and resisted, she would eventually die. This woman, however, stayed strong and faithful and told her husband, who confronted the sorcerer and threatened him with "hellfire" if he did not remove the spell. Though the sorcerer was intimidated by the husband, it did not quash his desires. To extract the love spell, the sorcerer ordered the woman to be locked in a hut with him. When the husband heard the screams of his wife, he rushed into the hut and found them mostly naked and in an uncompromising position. Thus, the sorcerer landed in court on attempted rape and eventually was given jail time. The husband and wife were still very concerned that the washing away of the spell was never completed. The woman worried that she would die. Periodically, the woman would travel to the hospital in Rabaul for a physical examination, and each time she was pronounced healthy, although her pulse would be slower than normal. Six months later, the woman died as her heart ceased to beat. An autopsy was performed, but the doctors found nothing unusual.

Beatrice Grimshaw did not shy away from writing about her sorcery experiences while traveling and living in Papua New Guinea. In her book *Isles of Adventure,* published in 1930, she admitted that she knew many sorcerers she described as "a reserved and cautious race." She believed that the sorcerers made the most imaginative masks and were the "best, the finest and most horrible. Some faces suggested the worst kind of nightmare, another, a jump-on-your-back little demon that is ugly enough to frighten any nervous person out of a night's sleep." On one occasion, Grimshaw was visiting a village in the Mekeo plain country and noticed a tall and powerful native with a huge bush of woolly hair teased out to an unusual size. The native was also painted with river mud that had dried white on his chest and legs. The significance of the mud meant that the sorcerer meant to kill someone, and the large frizzy hair concealed a poisonous snake coiled around the top of his head. Intimidated by his appearance, Grimshaw kept her distance and did not ask the sorcerer any questions lest he found her annoying.

Grimshaw continued to study the sorcerers of the Mekeo country and the unusual way they trained. She thought that the village of Mo was a kind of university for sorcerers that took about two years to complete their schooling. Nobody from the outside could learn what was going on during the training. However, by the end of the time, a young sorcerer emerged fully equipped to cause mayhem in the village. As Grimshaw put it, the sorcerers could,

"Curse a neighbor to death as easily as you or I could hail a taxicab. He could poison in secret ways; and could kill a man and bring him back to life again. He could use a private wireless system of immemorial antiquity that carries news where there was no apparent means of communication. He could see through things that are opaque to others. He could make himself invisible, and do things with poisonous snakes that no other snake-charmer would attempt."

Grimshaw added that everyone's life would be at risk if they offended a sorcerer and would most likely die by the bite of a snake. The sorcerers train their snakes by a secret process to bite anyone they wish, and that they would let the creatures loose at night near some crevice of the victim's house.

My favorite of Grimshaw's experiences showed the clairvoyant and smug side of the sorcerer. During a river flood, a boy from a Mekeo village was swept away and drowned. While the flood remained, there was no chance of finding the boy, but the parents planned to look for him as soon as it would be possible, in the place where such flotsam and jetsam were usually found. A white man was standing by the banks of a river, watching the mud-colored river rush past. He then spotted two sorcerers also watching the river. Intrigued, he walked towards them. "What are you looking at?" the white man calmly asked.

"The body of the youth," one of the sorcerers answered without looking at the white man.

"That's nonsense," the white man scoffed. "You can't see the boy through all this muddy water, plus it's impossible the boy should be in this part of the river at all." According to Grimshaw, sorcerers rarely argue. They smiled and pointed to the exact location where they believed the boy would be.

"There." The sorcerers then walked away. When the

waters finally receded, the boy's body was found precisely in the spot where the sorcerers said it would be.

More recent sorcery news has hit the front pages of newspapers throughout Melanesia and the Pacific, showing that Papua New Guinea still has a problem with the practice. The issues are flourishing across the entire country in villages, cities, squatter settlements, and districts where residents did not historically believe in sorcery. In 2018 one woman was killed, and two other women were critically injured after being tortured over sorcery allegations in the Kewabi area of the Southern Highlands province. An angry mob of villagers accused the three women of using sorcery to kill a man in the village. The women were tied up, placed on top of a heated aluminum sheet, and tortured before police intervened. Also, in the same year, a man who was blamed for the death of rugby league star Katto Ottio was attacked by an angry mob in the capital city of Port Moresby. Ottio was twenty-three and died unexpectedly during a training session. As the public waited for the post mortem results to be posted, rumors ran rife, especially on Facebook and throughout the country, to the point where it seemed that people talked themselves into advocating the cause of death to sorcery. In 2020 a woman and two boys were murdered by villagers from another village in the remote East Sepik region of the country. The three were blamed for using sorcery for a man's death earlier in the year. Finally, another report stated that a woman in Milne Bay was killed because she witnessed her father's death ten years earlier after being accused of practicing sorcery. The woman was killed because she was simply the oldest child of the accused sorcerer, and the perpetrators did not want her to take revenge.

As sorcery-related accusations, violence, and deaths

continue to occur into the present day in Papua New Guinea, there are organizations, stakeholders, and individuals trying to respond and put an end to this endemic problem. In 2014 the United Nations expressed deep concern about sorcery-related violence in the country and also believed that the violence against alleged sorcerers was a human rights issue. They set up a two-day meeting in Port Moresby and worked on strategies and approaches to implement a national action plan. The plan was presented to the Department of Justice and the Attorney General, hoping that they would endorse the recommendations to help alleviate the pressures of the issue of sorcery. In July 2015, the National Executive Council passed The Sorcery National Action Plan (SNAP) as one of the primary responses to abolishing the Sorcery Act of 1971. SNAP was an analytical policy document developed as an intervention strategy in response to the increased accounts of sorcery and sorcery-related violence. Its mission was to make Papua New Guinea a society free from sorcery-related violence through strengthened partnerships and committees among relevant stakeholders, especially in core hot spot provinces. These committees comprise a diverse group of champions such as relatives and neighbors of victims, police officers, church leaders, community activists, and leaders. SNAP was comprised of five core areas that included legal and protection, health, advocacy and communication, care and counseling, and research. Each area contained a few key recommendations and set out concrete activities to be taken in both the short and medium-term to implement the recommendations.

The Catholic Church has also taken an active role in combating sorcery and sorcery-related violence. Although the church believes in God, it also acknowledges the existence of evil and the reality of evil, which is sometimes conceived in terms of "evil spirits." The knowledge presented through science and rational argument is valued in the church. The church also believes that there are factual realities that can be perceived only with the "eyes of faith." Father Philip Gibbs, who is one of the leading advocates against the practice of sorcery in Papua New Guinea, agrees that people believe in sorcery as a way to cope with misfortune or loss and concludes that those fighting sorcery-related violence should try to understand what is really going on in people's minds, hearts, and their emotions. The Church plays a vital role at the local (village) level to deal with not just concepts but also with beliefs and emotions associated with life and death.

An example of this can be seen in the village of *Simbu*, where the Catholic Church has developed a plan with five related components. These include helping to broaden people's understanding of the causes of illness and death, intervening early before or during a funeral, having the immediate family members taking ownership and promoting peace, promoting respect for law and order, and fostering faith to influence attitudes and emotions. The plan has not entirely stopped sorcery in Simbu. However, there are encouraging signs where many sorcery accusations might have been made or where a situation could have exploded, but it did not. Other examples that the Catholic Church is doing to help address sorcery-related violence include forming response teams that work more closely with police, cooperating in many ways with implementing the Sorcery National Action Plan, and organizing workshops and forums that discuss the issues of sorcery. In fact, the Bishops have designated August 10 as International Day Against Sorcery Accusation Violence with the slogan, 'A Voice for the Voiceless.'

7
PRESERVING GHOSTS

In Melanesia, people feel that they are never alone on their islands and are in constant contact with ghosts, spirits, devils, and familiars. The world is full of magical, spiritual, and physical forces to be differentiated and controlled. For example, crops do not grow of their own accord, but the spirits that guard the gardens should be mollified or coaxed to ensure a bountiful harvest. Spirituality is a part of indigenous knowledge and is embedded in their traditional culture. It is holistic because information, skills, and values are rooted within a particular environment and separate from day-to-day living. It is not something one achieves, but rather it is the environment of society that shapes it. The spirituality of the Melanesians that percolates and trickles through the cycle of life within a web of relationships and experiences is orally passed down from ancestors from generation to generation. Spirituality is essential to traditional Melanesian societies because it helps them maintain a balanced relationship with the spirit world. Spirits need to be controlled or encouraged, and communities have men and women who specialize in certain kinds of magic. This includes magic that makes the community healthy and robust. It will make women fruitful, make yams grow, make the rain come and go, make a volcano erupt, and make people fall in love.

Traditional religion was not as formal as Christianity, and the relationship to supernatural beings that were part of their world gave their existence a sense that everything was related. While visiting villages along the Sepik River, Grimshaw noted in her observations about how the Papuans were "utterly given up to spiritism," which the white man could never understand. She wrote that the natives had what one may call the "feel" of the natives. "He can guess things; he can sense the existence of secrets, reserves, where the newcomer would see only blank, savage stupidity," Grimshaw added that what an outsider saw in the native and what one thought was the whole man may on any day, even after years of apparent intimacy, suddenly show itself to be only the surface. She witnessed a man who was no longer human and overheard midnight séances where things so incredible happened that she never dared to share them. "What is the deadly fascination of spiritism?- results! When an enquirer has savored that something, he is like a wild beast that has tasted blood, and he must have more." The impetus for life in a Melanesian society was a significant concern. Spirituality was a way for people to express their collective relationship to the spirits of the land, forest, mountains, rivers, animals, and birds.

Community is the most crucial element and of the highest value in Melanesian society. Everything is done to keep its balance and equilibrium. The experience of community is also integral to Melanesian spirituality. Although Melanesian culture involves special rites, gift exchanges, words, fighting, and killing, it is said that there were never disagreements, and everything is related and connected. Traditional beliefs influence the way the people in the community understand one another, and this is manifest through myths, stories, symbols, rituals, taboos, beliefs, arts, and dances.

Additionally, the community members' relationship with the spirit world traditionally mirrored people's exchanges with their families and other villagers. The pressure to maintain a harmonious relationship within the community could get overwhelming, especially if an unfortunate event happened to an individual or a group within the community. Thus, Melanesians feel a strong continuous element of fear that the spirits would punish them if customs and rituals were ever broken. This fear controlled the way they lived their lives and the relationships within the community. It is one of the reasons why the belief and practice of sorcery have been so embedded within the fragments of society. It was also one of the reasons why Christianity was able to gain an impregnable foothold in the region. Because the Melanesians had a connected and interactive relationship with good and evil spirits, the evangelists simply added God, Jesus, and the Devil to their supernatural beliefs.

For me, writing about community could not have come at a more significant time in the very early weeks of 2021, as the Covid-19 pandemic completely devastated the sense of community in the United States. In my state of California, the virus has now caused the deaths of 30,000 people. Even two gorillas at the San Diego Zoo have been diagnosed with the coronavirus. Fortunately, the two primates are only showing symptoms of sniffling and coughing. In my home area, the coyotes have definitely taken back the neighborhood, and I could have sworn I saw them late one night playing kickball against a team of raccoons in the cul-de-sac. But all joking aside, the number of deaths from Covid-19 within the U.S has hit a staggering 375,226. And to make matters worst, on January 6, a mob breached the U.S. Capitol building to interrupt and halt Congress from certifying the recent election results. The incident had been brewing for weeks. Horrifyingly, on the day of the riot, the mob was actually goaded by the President himself, who used phrases such as "never concede" and urged supporters "to fight." I joined millions of others, watching the unprecedented event unfold on television that left four dead (and others would die later by apparent suicide). The fate of democracy was at hand. I still wonder if it will survive. Community compromise was the undistinguished cornerstone of democracy, and after months of enduring the pandemic and watching the insurrection, I do not see the concept of community thriving anymore. Like the Melanesian's constant anxiety that controls the way they live, a sense of fear has crept into American society, making people shun and distrust one another. Our community will change, but for how long and how much will depend on the people themselves.

For Melanesians, the obligations to maintain peace and harmony within the community are very much linked to rituals. The faithful observance of a practiced performance is necessary as a means to tap into the supernatural to get what they want. Rituals are performed during important phases of a person's lifecycle and used to mend and renew broken relationships. Because Melanesians believe their world is integrated with the spirit world, rituals are essential. An example of this is seen in Papua New Guinea. If a woman becomes pregnant outside of marriage, it will bring shame to her family and relatives. Thus, before the baby is born, the woman must tell the midwife who the father is. Otherwise, labor will be prolonged, and problems could ensue. It could be fatal. The confession will ensure a safe and smooth delivery process.

Another example takes place in the East Sepik Province of Papua New Guinea, where villagers perform the sago dance that remembers the past, appreciates the present, and creates future relationships. Sago is a staple food and a primary source of carbohydrates. The community legend tells the story of a spirit that gives the villagers the sago plant. The dance is an expression of thankfulness to the spirit that gave them the sago.

Today, many of the rituals performed throughout Melanesia have become tourist attractions. One of the most popular rituals in Papua New Guinea is the Asaro Mudmen tradition deep in the Eastern Highlands. The most popular legend told about this ritual is that the Asaro people were once caught in the middle of a fierce tribal war. When one battle ended badly for them, the surviving Asaro people took cover on the banks of the Asaro River. The clay mud covered their entire bodies, which then dried to a shade of ghastly white. As the Asaro people made their escape during the night, the enemy was waiting for them. But when the enemy saw the whitened bodies rise from the riverbed, they looked like spirits from another realm. Frightened, the enemy ran away and forfeited the battle. From that day forward, imitating the spirits continues by creating masks of mud and replicating the movements that the spirits were said to have as a way of protecting their village.

On the island of Ambrym, known as the black magic

epicenter of Vanuatu, the Rom dance takes place—typically in July. The dances are set to the rhythmic beating of *tam-tams* (slit drums), strewn around a ceremonial dance ground. Seed shakers join the drums and dancers dressed in colorful leaves that feature tall conical banana fiber masks with flowing banana leaf capes. These leaf capes represent evil spirits. The masks are a symbol of power and are integral to a variety of ceremonies such as initiations and circumcisions. As the dance begins, stories, myths, legends, and beliefs entangled with the supernatural are told through chants that reflect the vast regional and cultural differences from all over the island of Ambrym.

In early September of 2017, I attended the Pacific Regional Branch of the International Council of Archives (PARBICA for short) conference at a resort in Pacific Harbour, which was in the southern part of the main island of Fiji Viti Levu. Since 2009, I have always made it a priority to attend these biennial events to look for new projects throughout the Pacific region, get together with colleagues, and meet new friends and colleagues. As a volunteer, who pays his own way to the conference, I found it easy to assimilate and make new islander friends. By contrast, I have always had a hard time with this in the U.S. In fact, one of the best compliments I have ever received and still cherish today was during a PARBICA conference in Samoa when a group of Pacific colleagues told me that I was "just like a Pacific Islander." Perhaps, it was the cool Bula Shirt that I was wearing at the time. Anyway, the weeklong conference always included a cultural visit that typically took place at a museum or a cultural or a traditional village. At this particular conference in Fiji, some attendees visited an Arts Village that was only a few minutes away from the conference hotel on Queens Road.

The village was somewhat of a tourist trap (with some sincerity) filled with stores selling Fijian products, clothing, and
food. In the middle of the village was a concert stand where
paying guests looked across a pond at a natural stage set-up
to look like a traditional Fijian village. It was by far the focal
point of the Arts Village. The performance was kind of the
typical Pacific show that tells the history and legends of the
island performed by very proud and passionate islanders. I
admit I was a little bored only because I have heard it all
before at other events. But then something happened, which I
had never seen before, that made me raise an eyebrow. It was
Fiji's legendary firewalkers.

The firewalking tradition has been around for five
hundred years. It comes from the highland village of
Nakarovu on Beqa Island, which was only six miles across the
lagoon of Pacific Harbour. The legend goes like this:

Seeking favor with a village elder, a young man named,
Tuinaiviqalita went in search of an eel to present as a gift.
Digging into a small hole near a creek, he grappled and
pulled out a slippery, writhing eel from its muddy hole.
When the creature cried out, the young man realized that
instead of an eel, he had captured one of Fiji's elusive little
people- a spirit god known locally as veli. The veli begged
Tuinaiviqalita for its freedom, promising him all kinds of
rewards, which he refused. Then, as a last-ditch effort, the
veli offered the young man and his descendants the power
over fire. Sensing Tuinaiviqalita's intrigue, the veli dug a
pit, lined it with river stones, and set them ablaze in a fire
until they turned white with heat. Then, leaping across the
smoldering stones, the veli beckoned the young man to
follow him. Tuinaiviqalita hesitantly stepped on the hot

stones and did not get burned. He knew that the veli was trustworthy and faithful to his word, and thus, let the spirit go.

Today, the power to walk on fire flows through Tuinaiviqalita's bloodline from the island of Beqa. After each man has conquered walking across the fiery pit, they end the ceremony with a chant and sacrifice their fern anklets known as *drau-ni-bala-bala*, which they throw into the pit. A few days later, they recover the anklets, grind and mix them into a tonic that is consumed by the firewalkers to complete the ritual. Before the firewalking begins, a long fern branch called a *waqa-bala-bala*, which is supposed to contain the spirit, is laid across the pit of coals to bless the fire.

Fijian Fire Walkers, Pacific Harbour, Fiji

For me, sitting in the stands and watching the extraordinary show, I looked at my own prissy feet, knowing full well I could not do much without some kind of protection on them. I have seen islanders play soccer on a coral beach, trample up rugged mountain paths and now walk on fire in

their bare feet without a care in the world. A million thoughts
ran through my mind. I wondered how and when the original
ritual of walking on fire took place on the island of Beqa. I
wondered if they saw the spirits rise from the hot stones and
what the missionaries thought when they first saw this ritual.
I even wondered what the islanders walking on the burning
pit in front of me did after the show. Most of all, I wondered
what I could not see in this ritual. Are rituals only a show
now? What I did not see I could not understand, or vice-versa.
My attention was lost in thought, as usual, and I did not snap
out of it until I heard the distinct clamor of clapping. The
show had ended.

Throughout Melanesia, there was a belief that spirits
could either harm or help a person. Children were taught at a
very early age to be wary of spirits and how powerful and
harmful they could be. They were told to stay away from any
suspected places or objects that were believed to be the territory of the spirits and that the spirits could manifest in a
variety of ways. In the Solomon Islands, for example, village
women would rush their children inside the house whenever
they heard the call of the *korokoro* bird because they believed
that the bird's call meant that someone was about to be
harmed. Children also learned to return home before
sundown because it was believed that the most effective and
restless time for spirits was at night. Although the world
seemed to include fearful ghosts, Melanesians also turned to
benevolent spirits, especially to help them when evil and
vengeful spirits tried to do harm. Anything associated with
goodness, such as catching bountiful fish, was thought to be a
friendly spirit aiding them with the successful catch. The
Melanesian went nowhere, did nothing, and planned nothing
without some kind of sacrifice, and prayer, to the spirits that

constantly lived among them. Be that as it may, the belief in good and evil spirits throughout the region could be characterized into three distinct categories. These were spirits associated with the ancestors, nature, and death.

The ancestors are the pillar and foundation of Melanesian society, and islanders rely on ancestral knowledge to understand the world. In most societies around the globe, people have looked to their grandparents for venerable knowledge and sagacious advice. In Melanesia, however, it is a little more profound because the ancestors are responsible for building the spiritual worldviews and cultures. In turn, they have become the spiritual guardians of their descendants.

A traditional Melanesian village

The ancestral spirits act as the maps that guide people and lead them into the unknown. George Mombi, a Lecturer and the Associate Dean of the Christian Leaders Training College in Papua New Guinea, believes that Melanesians "enter life with their backs to the future, and look to their ancestral heritage to gain understanding to face the future." Ancestral spirits control life. They have superior knowledge and the power to make things happen. They are always invisibly present.

The belief in the presence of ancestral spirits is often supported by natural and fantastical encounters. Mombi once shared a personal story highlighting the belief in ancestral spirits in a paper he wrote for a theology journal. When he was a boy, his grandfather and his father told him that the spirits of the dead were all around him and were quite visible. Mombi's father added that some of his uncles had encounters with a visible dead spirit of one of their relatives who had died during childbirth. It was thought that ghosts who manifested visibly were typically unfriendly. One of the reasons the townspeople in Mombi's village built their houses on high posts with mobile ladders was to keep the visible dead out of the house at night. He recalled that one day all the visible dead spirits disappeared and were never seen again. Over the years, Mombi wondered about this disappearance. He thought that, perhaps, the spirits of the dead relatives and ancestors allowed themselves to clearly manifest to the villagers in their exact human forms until the time came for their departure to an unspecified, unknown place.

The belief and respect given to ancestral spirits was shown in the architecture of historic and contemporary buildings throughout Melanesia. The architecture varied depending on climate, landscape, and available materials and was linked with culture and religion. For example, in Papua New Guinea, spirit houses, or *haus tambaran*, were traditionally constructed with timber, bamboo, coconut leaf, and other materials and were often built on stilts over land or water. They generally had elaborately decorated front walls and a sweeping pitched roof. These houses were reserved for initiated men only and were characterized by a large trussed entrance and no windows to ensure privacy during ceremonies.

The spirit houses also served as a cultural and spiritual meeting area and were used to store sacred objects. The more modern Parliament House in Port Morseby was built to replicate a *haus tambaran*. Another example could be found in New Caledonia, where the chief's house was considered both the physical and metaphorical center of every Kanak village. The houses were typically circular, with towering conical roofs crowned with carved roof spires called *flèche faîtière*. This type of spire symbolized the presence of the ancient and highly worshipped ancestors. The central face of these carved spires represented the ancestral spirits, which were symbolic of the community of the spirits of the departed and the transition between the worlds of the dead and the living. When the chief died, the spire was placed on top of his grave or in some specific memorial location appropriate for his clan to visit.

There was a time in Fiji when large villages constructed spirit houses as a place of ancestral worship. These houses would eventually be displaced starting in 1835 when the missionaries came and the islanders converted to Christianity. These spirit houses, however, were typically a place where the chief of the village consulted the spirits of the ancestors through a medium of a priest, who usually lived in the house and whom the spirit was believed to possess during the time of consultation. Today, models of the spirit house can be found only in museums. And although people of the Fijian society show little interest in spirit houses these days, the guidance of ancestral spirits remains as strong and desirable as ever before.

———

In 2006 before I embarked on an archival career, and certainly before I created ICAS, I happened by chance to get a volunteer position at the Vanuatu National Library for a couple of weeks. This was even before they acquired the National Archives. I was looking for a place to volunteer mainly on one of the Polynesian islands when a Melanesian Librarian at the University of California San Diego recommended I contact Anne at the National Library in Vanuatu. With a staff of two and a backlog of work, Anne was more than excited for me to come and help out. I admit, at first, I was not greatly thrilled to go to Vanuatu. In fact, I did not even know where Vanuatu was. When I saw that it was in Melanesia, I had some reservations about working in a developing country where it was possible to pick up malaria and other odd diseases. But then I thought that this was all part of the adventure. The Melanesian Librarian told me that Vanuatu was a beautiful place with lovely, smiling people and that I would love it. She said the country was the best-kept secret in the Pacific. She was right. It was simply Heaven on earth. Every time I left, I could not wait for the next opportunity to return. And every time I did go back, another adventure was waiting for me.

Melanesia, and especially Vanuatu's *kastom*, was truly foreign to me. Although it was a very different world than what I was used to, I came to adjust my western way of thinking quickly and accepted the unusual custom practices. The nakamal (kava bars) throughout the town were truly mysterious to me. They served as a type of pub for ni-Vanuatu and visitors, primarily male, where they typically gathered at night. The Chief's *Nakamal* sat in the same park as the Cultural Center where the library was located and was only about fifty yards away. This particular *nakamal* was a rather large ornate building, as opposed to most of them, which were actually small bamboo-walled, tin-roofed shelters that seemed to fit no more than ten people at a time. But it was in these dilapidated dwellings that kava was shared as a gateway to the supernatural realm where men would hear the voices of their ancestors.

The Chief's Nakamal, Port Vila, Vanuatu

During this visit in 2006, I passed a couple of *nakamals* on my way from my boarding room to the library. I remember as I was making my way back to my room on one dark, late after-noon, I had an urge to peer into one of these spiritual places. I stopped at a *nakamal* and stared at it for a spell, thinking that a strong gust of wind would blow the structure over. It took me several minutes to muster enough courage actually to look inside. Finally, I just did it. I opened the door and looked inside, but it was too dark to see anything except for two pairs of white eyes looking at me as if they knew I was coming. It took me by surprise. I quickly pardoned myself and closed the door. Who was I to disturb their moment talking with their dead relatives? Now, I have no doubt they would have shared *kava* with me, but at the time, I kind of lived a pre-pandemic life as if I was already living in the middle of a worldwide virus outbreak. Do not get me wrong. I am not a prude. But that ramshackle shack did not appear to be very hygienic, and I just did not want to get sick. If you have ever been sick in a foreign, developing country, you know what I mean.

Because Melanesians have such a close relationship with the land, the belief in nature spirits plays an integral part in the people's lives. These spirits can be classified into two groups: roaming spirits and spirits that attach themselves to a particular place or object such as a forest, lake, river, swamp, cave, mountain, rock, sago palm patches, etc. Although nature spirits can be friendly or malevolent, the stories often include a spirit with a more sinister, vengeful purpose. Nighttime, especially, is when nature spirits roamed the land, and if any man is out after dark, there is a good chance that he will encounter a spirit.

Indeed, when Williamson was staying in a village in the highlands of Espiritu Santo, Vanuatu, he noted in his book *Cavorting with Cannibals* that if the screech of a nighthawk (owl) was heard flying overhead at night, it was a sign of impending doom. If the bird was heard flying outside nearby, nobody was allowed to go out of the hut until daybreak. Williamson added that no one ever dared to leave the sanctity of the hut, even to go to the toilet. "If I needed to relieve myself, I was to go in the corner of the hut rather than dashing outside, which would result in my certain death when the spirit within the nighthawk attacked me." Most spirit-fearing people believe that the ghosts are most active during heavy rains or in the early part of the evening from sunset to about ten o'clock and then again towards daybreak.

The islanders in this region know the taboo territories. If they do enter these areas, they may quite well receive capital punishment by the spirit. There was a story from the Solomon Islands about a policeman who treated the people of a particular village so badly that they decided to lead him into a malicious spirit's territory. One day a few of the villagers enticed him to go hunting for birds with them. Nothing would have happened to him if he had not asked the villagers where he could relieve himself. They pointed him to a giant tree believed to be the resting place of a vengeful spirit. The policeman went to the tree and relieved himself. Later in the evening, while at home, he felt a headache coming on. As he laid down to rest, he saw a tall angry spirit standing over him with a club in his hand. The club dropped onto his head. Later that night, he died.

Melanesians believe that the presence of nature spirits can be sensed, especially out in the bush. Many ghosts can cry, appear in strange or hilarious human form, and change, at any time, into an animal. When these unusual happenings occur, it could mean injury or death either to a person who meets a spirit or a relative in the village. Thus, being sensitive to the environment can be an advantage. Penuel Idusulia, who was head of the New Testament Studies at Atomea Memorial School in Mahluu, North Malaita Province in the Solomon Islands, wrote that four signs could detect the presence of spirits:

1. The crying of the *keke* insect when a passing spirit disturbs the sleeping bug;
2. The deafening of one's ears, as though one receives a punch on his head;
3. The hair on the body standing on end; and
4. The passing ghost may tap the trunk of a tree, which a person can hear.

Spirits who attach themselves to a particular object will remain attached to that object. It is a prerequisite that a prescribed ritual is performed to appease the ghost if an object is moved. If not, the spirit will become enraged and bring harm to the trespasser.

Mombi told an interesting story about a time when he returned home to Biwat village along the Yuat River in the East Sepik Province of Papua New Guinea. Because his village was along the river, the villagers relied on canoes for travel. Mombi's family needed a new canoe, so he and some of his kin felled a long enough tree to make two canoes. As they were crafting the canoe, the Yuat River was overflowing. His mother prepared food for the workmen, and three of his sisters traveled inland to bring the lunch to the workmen. To avoid the flooded bush tracks, the sisters decided to travel along another path on higher ground. As they made their way inland, they came upon a large death adder sleeping on the pathway. With fear, they called out to some youths from another village, making their way home, to kill the snake. When the youths killed the snake, a huge pig jumped out from the bush and took off into the jungle. Later that night, Mombi's elder sister had a dream that the snake was not just a snake but rather, it was a nature spirit. Mombi's sister dreamt that she saw the relatives of the nature spirit appear with dirt rubbed over their bodies mourning the deceased snake. These relatives in the dream told Mombi's sister that the youths had killed one of their kin and gave her the names of three female relatives of the snake. The three names were Kunetrengbe, Gindakpe and Sarikpe. Ironically, two of Mombi's deceased nieces were named Kunetrengbe and Sarikpe, respectively.

Spirits associated with death must be evaluated by whether or not they are to be feared or are determined harmless. The spirits of those who have recently died are deemed to be the most active and dynamic. The existence of the dead seemed to be dependent on the memory of the living. In fact, 'fear' has been a noticeable component in Melanesian spirituality and can control how a person lives his life or associates with others. As ghosts of ordinary people are often a cause of anxiety, the relationship between Melanesians and the supernatural can be driven by a strong element of fear. For example, the fear of breaking *kastom*, or a ritual, will result in being punished by a spirit.

After the separation of soul and body in death, a person's soul will become a ghost, and every death is upsetting to the entire village at the time. The most feared spirits are dead sorcerers, those who are murdered, those who died in childbirth, suicide, or accidental deaths. These ghosts will become restless, uneasy, and most likely need much appeasing. For example, a crying child is always accompanied by a dead mother's spirit, and the mother can often be heard trying to make sounds to quiet the child. A jealous wife or husband will sometimes commit suicide so that the ghost or spirit would be free to take vengeance for the wrong he or she was too feeble or unable to exact on earth.

The spirits of a hanged man are also highly feared by villagers. Penuel Idusulia wrote about a particular belief in his village that a person's eyes could be altered to see evil spirits. He could recall one man who had his eyes changed, but he could not stand the sight of the ghosts after some time. He eventually had his eyes treated again to give him normal eyesight. Be that as it may, the whole Melanesian world teemed with ghostly influences, and their minds were filled with a sense of the unseen powers which entwined and determined even the most minute aspects of life on earth.

Melanesian's relationship to supernatural beings will also give meaning to their livelihood and their sense of identity. Ghosts exercise significant power over the living, and the living often try to win the ghost's favor by prayer and sacrifice. The Reverend Dr. R.H. Codrington, a very observant missionary in Melanesia, particularly in the Solomon Islands, for twenty-four years from 1864 to 1887, wrote that a man's natural powers and capabilities were regarded as a supernatural inheritance acquired by communications with the spirit world. He cited the example that "if a man is a great warrior, it is not because he is strong of arm, quick of eye, or brave of heart, it is because he is supported by the ghost of a dead warrior whose power he has drawn to himself through an amulet of stone tied around his neck, or a tuft of leaves in his belt, or a tooth attached to one of his fingers, or a spell by the recitation of which he can enlist the aid of a ghost."

While working on a project at the National Archives of the Solomon Islands in 2012, I had the unfortunate experience of being in the wrong place at the wrong time. It was around noon when I was in the repository shelving boxes of the collection that we were preserving. The monotonous hum of the sole air conditioning unit filled the room, which had no windows and only one door that the staff religiously kept closed to keep the cool air from escaping. As I reached to place a box on the shelf, the power to the building snapped off. I was left standing in pitch darkness. Now, the archives building always lost power every day in the afternoon, and it would sometimes return within a couple of minutes, or it would take a couple of hours. One never knew how long it would take to restore power. I stood frozen, hoping that the lights would turn back on and wishing I had a flashlight. The room quickly became still and quiet; the heat and humidity of the day slowly crept inside like a burglar. I knew which direction the door was, but navigating some of the shelving was tricky. As I slowly felt my way to the door like a blind man, I kicked something on the floor that made me stop. It was most likely that I stumbled over a stack of oversized books that were too large to find space on the shelves. But as I side-stepped the books, something like a hand patted me on my back. I quickly turned around. Of course, I saw nothing, but I asked, "Who is there?" There was no answer.

Half of the archivist's profession is preserving the memory of ghosts, while the other half is trying to prepare the living peoples' legacy for that day when they do become ghosts. But, on this day in the pitch blackness of the repository, it was not the time to feel the hand of appreciation. An odd, eerie feeling came over me in the darkness. The humidity wrapped me like a hug, and I started sweating. At this point, I did not care what I was going to bump into as I determinedly went for the door and followed a small ray of light that beamed through a crack in the door. I stumbled out of the door and into the conservation room where Kabini was still cleaning documents using the natural light from the windows. Bernard was also in the room engrossed in his laptop. I stood there staring at the two for a second and then asked, "Did you guys notice anyone come into the repository?" Kabini shrugged his shoulders and shook his head negatively. Bernard said he had not seen anyone. I looked back at the repository door and waited for someone to exit. Nobody did. I then turned back to the guys and said, "I'm going to get something to eat." I took a longer lunch than usual that day.

8

DARK TOURS

Visiting a cemetery for a funeral or simply remembering those loved ones who have already gone to the afterlife can be an emotional event. Some cemeteries lack adequate paths, or the plots are extremely close together, thus forcing one to tiptoe or awkwardly leap across the hallowed ground to get to the desired gravesite. When accidentally stepping on someone's grave, it feels taboo with the possibility of bad luck befalling the trespasser. Whenever I have found myself in this situation, I try to make a conscientious effort to respect the gravesite and not walk on it. When tiptoeing around a plot like an uncoordinated ballerina, it is inevitable to misstep and plop a foot on the grave. I then imagine a hand breaking through the earth and grabbing my ankle or a grave's ghost following me home to punish me. This is the last thing that I need. But the dead can still have opinions, and who am I to disrespect them? Even the few battlefields that I have visited, such as Gettysburg, I wondered if I was stepping on the very spot where a soldier fell mortally wounded.

It was easy to feel like I was trudging on someone's grave while on the island of Guadalcanal, Solomon Islands, especially in and around Honiara. Some of the fiercest and most gruesome fighting during World War Two took place there in 1942. Over 7,000 Americans were killed in a six-month period, and the number of dead Japanese soldiers, incredibly, tripled the number of U.S. soldiers. The entire island became a memorial to those who fought and continues to hold an important part in the Solomon Islands' history. Places like Iron Bottom Sound, Betikama, Mbonegi, Henderson Airfield (which is the international airport today), Bloody Ridge, Alligator Creek, and the Matanikau River have become hallowed ground in this tropical, tranquil landscape. Visiting these places, I came to understand that I was not just stepping on someone's grave. I was stepping on a killing field.

It is also impossible to forget the war as reminders of the battles are strewn throughout these island nations. In 2019, The New Zealand Defense Force Bomb Disposal Team helped collect and destroy over 1,000 unexploded World War Two munitions in the Solomon Islands on land and at sea. Upon arriving at a small coastal village, a child mentioned to the disposal team that she knew an area where some potential unexploded ordinances were. The team followed the girl about three kilometers into the jungle and, to their surprise, found a Japanese 70mm anti-aircraft gun position with three guns intact. They also found that placed around the gun were three live 70mm high explosives shells and one hand grenade.

The country was littered with unexploded ordinances, and since the war, dozens of people have been killed or maimed by the munitions. The Solomon Islands Ordinance Disposal Team often conducted live demolition of the bombs. In July of 2019, with assistance from the police, the team warned the

Guadalcanal citizens that old bombs were set to be detonated at Hells Point near the Alligator River. In this area, a large number of collected bombs were stored. Over the years, these unusual warnings have occurred quite frequently. More recently, in September 2020, a horrific news story broke. Two aid workers from Australia and Great Britain were mapping a deadly legacy of unexploded munitions from World War Two. Suddenly a bomb on which they were working detonated and killed them both.

Despite the continued dangers of unexploded bombs, these World War Two sites are morbid fields of death and destruction. Yet somehow they are becoming popular tourist destinations. The Solomon Islands are not just a place where intrepid divers endure long flights for a top-notch underwater experience. Tourists, cruisers, and World War Two buffs are now arriving to learn and see first-hand the areas where the two armies slugged it out. *The Thin Red Line*, The 1999 Academy Awards nominated World War Two film, was partially filmed on Guadalcanal and has attracted tourists who want to see some of the lush areas where the filming took place. Indeed, visiting battlefields has proved to be quite popular worldwide. It is not about stepping on a potential fallen soldier's grave. Instead, it is about immersing oneself in the horrors and struggles of those involved in the historic event. It is known as Dark Tourism, where some tourists do not even associate a place of death with anything other than a tourist destination. Others simply need to visit a grim place to understand it better. The Guadalcanal campaign of World War Two has put the Solomon Islands on the Dark Tourism map.

Dark Tourism, also called grief tourism or black tourism, is a type of tourism that involves traveling to places that are historically associated with tragedy and death. These tourist sites are directly or indirectly related to death. They include places of executions and mass exterminations, murders, battlefields, prisons, slavery, paranormal, and areas affected by environmental disasters like hurricanes, tsunamis, and volcano eruptions. Travelers attracted to dark tourism sites are typically interested in the cultural and historical aspects of the places. They prefer to visit the sites instead of reading about them in books. When the dark tourism site is promoted and run ethically and respectfully, it can expose travelers to a broader understanding of the country they are visiting, challenge perceptions, and have the power to inspire. Professor John Lennon, director of the Moffat Centre for Travel and Tourism at Glasgow Caledonian University, believes "It's a crucial way for us all to learn the lessons of our past. To remain silent and not record and interpret these events for tourists may encourage future generations to ignore or forget these terrible periods of human history. Dark Tourism, like our dark history, occupies an important part of our understanding of what it is to be human." Even though the term "death" is grim and negative, it is the main factor that drives this type of tourism. Many people are fascinated to understand this term because the concept of death is inevitable and cannot be conquered.

Several factors perpetuate the desire to explore these kinds of bleak places. Sometimes there is a personal connection, yet more often, a morbid fascination or a sense of social responsibility might cause a person to add these places to their "bucket list" or "must-see" sites. Others may prefer them for religious and spiritual reasons, retrospection, adventure-seeking, risks, and thrills. Some find the need to become acquainted with a place that has had a tragedy, choosing to learn about a site with immortal memories linking oneself to a place of historical importance. Empathy also plays a significant role—relying on the visitor's ability to know the stories that have taken place at a particular location. For example, people will visit the Auschwitz-Birkenau Concentration Camp in Poland to better understand what their relatives experienced. Some of the top dark tourism sites are Ground Zero-the 9/11 Memorial in New York City, Hiroshima Peace Memorial Park in Japan, Alcatraz Federal Penitentiary in San Francisco, the Island of Dolls in Mexico, and even a Jack the Ripper Tour in London, to name a few. One can easily play a game trying to name all of the dark tourism sites worldwide.

It has only been about fifteen to twenty years ago when the term "dark tourism" came to be, but believe it or not, the fascination with visiting morbid places of death has been around for centuries. Many people embarked on pilgrimages to sites of martyrdom and public executions. The Roman gladiatorial games at the Colosseum might be considered one of the earliest dark tourism sites. People traveled long distances to become spectators of a sport that involved a lot of death. Between the seventeenth and nineteenth centuries, many people visited places such as Pompeii, or the grounds of the Battle of Waterloo, to experience the tragic events that took place there. Even Victorian-era mental institutions were favorite spots for the wealthy elite to come and ogle subjectively the clinically insane. It was not until 1996 that the term "dark tourism" was coined. Two academics from Glasgow applied it while looking at sites associated with the assassination of John F. Kennedy in Dallas, Texas. Today, at least in the pre-pandemic times, this type of tourism has grown in popularity and has become truly dramatic travel, thought-provoking, educational and macabre.

The Pacific Islands also offer many dark tourism sites that attract thousands of visitors each year. Pearl Harbor in Hawaii is a melancholy, morbid memorial of the surprise Japanese attack on the U.S. Navy fleet in December 1941 that brought the Americans into World War Two. Today, visitors need to make an appointment to visit the *USS Arizona*, where over 1,100 men lost their lives and went down with the ship. As a United States' nuclear bomb testing site, which included the hydrogen bomb detonation, between the years 1945 to 1958, the Bikini Atoll in the Marshall Islands has become uninhabited except for it being a "must" destination for extreme divers. Many tourists travel long hours to visit a couple of gravesites on the island of Hiva Oa in the Marquesas Islands of French Polynesia. The two graves belong to famous French artists—Paul Gaugin and the singer, songwriter, actor, director Jacques Brel. Eastern Island, which today belongs to Chile, is a spot where visitors arrive to learn about how a lost civilization whose collapse is quite similar to the environmental issues the world is experiencing today. These islands in the Pacific region are some of the most remote places on earth, yet people find ways to travel there to experience unique cultures and history.

As Melanesia becomes a more popular tourist destination, it provides its share of dark places to visit. Many are attracting people with extraordinary cultural practices of the past or the actions of the colonial governments. For example, in 1872, France established a penal colony in New Caledonia, and by 1897 over 21,000 people would be registered in the various penitential centers on the archipelago. Communard deportees were sent to the Isle of Pines following the revolution period known as the 'Commune of Paris' in 1871. Although overrun by foliage, a few ruins remain. The cemetery is still maintained and attracts numerous visitors who want to see the predominantly anonymous graves of the convicts who died.

On Fiji's largest island of Viti Levu, many thrill-seeking tourists cannot pass up the chance to visit the Naihehe Cave. The last known cannibal tribes of Fiji used this underground cave system, which is over five hundred feet long. Naihehe means 'the place to get lost' and was often the place villagers hid from marauding cannibal tribes. In the past, one would have to float along the Sigatoka River on a bamboo raft to a trail, then hike to reach the cave's entrance. Today, the cave still contains a cannibal oven, a ritual platform, a sacred priest chamber, and other reminders of its cannibal history.

The land diving ceremony on Pentecost Island, Vanuatu, can also be considered a dark tourism spot. When the men jump from the towers, there are no nets, cushions, or safety equipment to soften their fall. If the vines that support the ankles break, it could result in broken bones or even death. When Britain's Queen Elizabeth visited Vanuatu in 1974, when Britain governed the archipelago, islanders from Pente-cost put on a diving show for her. Unfortunately, it was the wrong time of the year. The vines they used were dry; thus, they snapped. Several divers smashed against the ground, and one of them later died from his injuries.

The author Beatrice Grimshaw was most likely the first person to create an interest in dark tourism in Melanesia in the very early part of the twentieth century. Although she produced a plethora of published fiction pieces, she also wrote at least three nonfiction books and two travel brochures titled "The Islands of the Blest" and "Three Wonderful Nations," respec-tively. The publication dates of these brochures are uncertain. However, all her nonfiction work had two distinct objectives:

to attract escapism to Polynesia and to endorse settlement and tourism in Melanesia.

In her 1907 publication title, *From Fiji to the Cannibal Islands*, Grimshaw's prose was seemingly directed at prospective settlers and was used to spark tourism in Fiji. The descriptions of her horseback journey through the center of Fiji, which could also be found in *"Three Wonderful Nations,"* were also used to promote settlement and ethnic tourism to the Fiji islands. In her other travel accounts through Vanuatu's forests or along the Papuan rivers, the seeds of ethnic adventurous tourism would explode in popularity well into the twentieth-first century.

Grimshaw's attitude and description of the islanders were quite brutal by today's standards. Her comments ranged from patronizing to disgusted, but her school of thought towards the islanders was rationalized by what would be known as 'social Darwinism.' This was the theory that human groups and races were subject to the same laws of natural selection as Charles Darwin perceived in plants and animals in nature. After seeing a Fijian making fire by rubbing two sticks together, Grimshaw commented in *From Fiji to the Cannibal Islands:* "It was my first example of the truth that the Fijian civilization is only varnish deep. Cannibalism has been abandoned, cruelty and torture given up, and an ample amount of clothing universally adopted. Yet, the Fijian of 1905, freed from the white control that moulded his life, would spring back like an unstrung bow to the thoughts and ways of his fathers. This is a truth doubted by no one who knew the inner life of Fiji." Grimshaw believed settlers were necessary to bring fulfillment and nobility to the Pacific Islands.

The same perspective—bringing settlers and tourists especially to New Guinea—would also be Grimshaw's desire.

After all, she lived there for twenty-seven years. Although the country was a British colony, it was far from settled, and as late as 1903, there had been violent massacres of settlers by natives. In 1907 Grimshaw secured passaged on the steamer, *Merrie England*, to New Guinea. Coupled with another trip in 1909, which detailed in her travel, she would publish *The New New Guinea* in 1910. More than any of her other nonfiction works, this book was partially intended as a resource book for potential visitors to New Guinea. It focused on the capacity to sustain the indigenous population. She was concerned with the interaction of land and people, especially how the former supports the latter. This was the complete opposite of what the islander would think. Nevertheless, the book would receive more favorable reviews than the other of Grimshaw's travelogues, and a *New York Times* article written by Forbes Lindsay praised "the lifelike pictures of the native tribes and charming descriptions of the country." No doubt, this piqued the interest of future travelers to the region.

Although Grimshaw was not an ethnographer or a geographer, her many accounts of the ethnological "other" and her descriptions of landscape would be accepted by a wide readership. Throughout her nonfiction pieces, the imagery of the indigenous dark, and sometimes macabre, cultural practices were quite numerous. She was conscious that there was a market for horror among those who may travel to Papua as tourists. Thus, she was very aware of the marketability of death. Her writing often approached cannibalism, sorcery, and headhunting in a very apathetic and detached tone. While visiting a village along the Sepik River, Grimshaw trades for a head as if it was a souvenir. She wrote, "Heads were plenty—a woman's among them, with short black curls on the dried scalp; a child's head or two; men's heads cleverly worked up, with modeled and painted clay faces and eyes of shell or mother-of-pearl. I asked if any were to be bought." The villagers would not sell any heads, but they had no compunction about trading one for a knife. Grimshaw had qualms about buying a human skull for the price of a knife.

Grimshaw's experience and writing constructed a type of dark tourism in Melanesia. When describing a skull rack in a Papuan temple, Grimshaw wrote, "It was about a foot wide by twenty feet long, and was set with a row of teeth. On every fork a skull was spiked; it was painted red, white and black in a sort of snake pattern, and was clearly the first object of interest in the place." This temple offered the tourist a spectacle and merchandising—one may stare at death and then purchase a symbol of his own survival and mortality. Professor Emeritus at the University of California Davis and author Dean MacCannell wrote that mortality became a preoccupation among the traveling classes in the second half of the nineteenth century. He also argued that the exercise in visual consumption was really an attempt to consolidate the tourist's conception of self. The tourist observes death, yet "it is death of the other death occurring at someone else's body." When Grimshaw traded for the head, she was affirming her position as a survivor, and it was a death of the "other" in a more decorated and aesthetic representation.

Today, Papua New Guinea is a mysterious and timeless country visited by people looking for extreme off-the-beaten-path adventures. The jungle is home to many distinct ethnic groups often hidden from modern society in dense flora. There are tribal communities that have only recently been in contact with the outside world. These tribes are famous for their ornate woodcarvings and for being legendary cannibals and headhunters. Visitors can undertake extreme, dark expeditions to get more of an inside glimpse at these mystifying and enigmatic communities. The local government grants about a hundred permits annually for people to visit villages in the Asmat region of the tidal swamplands of West Papua's southern coast.

The Asmats were also infamous for allegedly killing and eating Michael Rockefeller, the great-grandson of the world's first billionaire, John D. Rockefeller. After an initial scouting trip to collect the art of the Asmat people, the twenty-three-year-old Michael, accompanied by a government anthropologist named René Wassing, returned a second time in November of 1961. As their boat approached the village of Otsjanep, a sudden squall capsized them, leaving Michael and René clinging to the overturned boat. Despite René's supplications not to swim ashore, Michael swam the twelve miles to the shore and was never seen again. Speculation as to what happened to Michael remains a topic of debate to this date. Some people said a shark or a crocodile ate him. Others thought he was still living in the jungle. However, most people believe that he was most likely killed and eaten by cannibals to restore balance to their world. Because the Asmat people had very limited contact with the outside world at the time, they believed the land beyond their island to be inhabited by spirits. When white people came, they saw them as some kind of supernatural beings full of *mana*. In the days before Michael swam to the shore, a "tribe of white men" had killed four villagers, and it is believed that they felt it was time for retribution. Thus, by consuming the body of Michael Rockefeller, they could absorb the *mana* that had been taken from them.

Another example of a modern, dark tourist expedition in Papua New Guinea is visiting The Chambri Tribe along the

Sepik River. This region is known for being the home of the world's largest freshwater and saltwater crocodiles. The men of the Chambri Tribe are also known as the "Crocodile Men of Papua New Guinea" and believe that humans evolved from the prehistoric predators and are, therefore, sacred. The crocodile is the symbol of strength, power, and manhood. To make the transition from boy to man, males aged eleven to thirty years old take part in a body mutilation ceremony. Elders of the village make the skin appear scaly like a crocodile from the shoulders to the hips. The elders use bamboo slivers to make hundreds of deep slices into the male's flesh during the ceremony. After the skin cutting is complete, the males sit close to a fire where the smoke is blown into the wounds. Then clay and tree oil are applied to the cuts to ensure the scars remain raised once they heal. At the end of the ceremony, the males participate in tribal rituals and are then considered to have reached the status of a man and crocodile. Although it is not a ceremony for the meek, the intrepid tourist could travel to Ambunti, East Sepik Province, to witness this unusual ritual during the first weekend of August.

During my first visit to Vanuatu in 2006, I had the opportunity to visit Chief Roi Mata's Domain, which consisted of three seventeenth-century sites of the islands Efate, Lelepa, and Artok- also known as Hat Island. While working at the National Library in the Vanuatu Culture Center, a week-long Anthropology Conference took place. The group took a field trip to Chief Roi Mata's Domain on the weekend, and Anne thought it would be a terrific opportunity for me to tag along. As I did not have a lot of money with me, it was fortunate that the trip was economical and included a big feast at the end. Thus, on a cloudy Saturday morning, I crowded into a small bus with a bunch of inquisitive anthropologists from around the world. The driver's adroit attempts to avoid the rather large potholes highlighted the hour drive from Port Vila. I mean, these holes were like ground monsters with giant mouths ready to swallow a car whole. The American servicemen built the road that encircles Efate Island during World War Two, and now, it was desperately in need of repair.

Along the way, the anthropologists got very excited at the different tropical foliage within the jungle and were especially interested in the number of pandanus trees growing in the bush. Like the coconut tree in the region, the pandanus tree was also considered a tree of life. They provided materials for housing, clothing, textiles, mats, rope, decorations, fishing, religious use, and edible fruit. I personally thought the fruit looked like something from outer space. But I have to admit that the ones I ate on the Polynesian island of Tuvalu were quite sweet and tasty. Once we got to our destination, a couple of boats were ready to take us across to Lelepa Island.

Roi Mata was a dominant and influential thirteenth-century Melanesian chief in Vanuatu, who united various tribes and whose reign was believed to be one of peace and harmony. Historians credit him for leading a social revolution that helped to dissolve the tribal system of Vanuatu. In fact, his peacekeeping strategies are still used today, which has helped preserve the chiefly title system. Chiefs in Vanuatu still hold a critical role within society. However, oral history said that Chief Mata died after being poisoned by his brother. Fearing that Mata's spirit would haunt the land he was killed on, he was buried on Artok Island. He was not buried alone on this island as fifty members of his family were sacrificed and buried near him so that they could all travel together to the next world. Scores of his followers, confidantes, and advisors were also buried alive in pits around Mata's grave. Most of

these people volunteered and sedated themselves on strong
kava or were clubbed to death and pushed into the pit. The
exact number of people who joined Mata was unknown, but
some historians believe it could be as many as three hundred.
For centuries after his burial, the island was taboo for ni-
Vanuatu and closed for everyone else per local tradition
prohibiting the area's intensive use. In 2008 the United
Nations Educational, Scientific and Cultural Organization
(UNESCO) had designated the island as well as the Roi Mata
Domain as a heritage site. Today, cultural tours are available
for tourists to visit the domain, as it provides an income for
the local communities and educates visitors about the culture
and history of the area. This includes a visit to the gravesite of
Roi Mata, where two large stones are placed for him and his
wife. Smaller stones surround them, which represent all the
other people buried there.

A Vanuatu seascape with Hat Island in the backdrop

By the time the anthropologist group and I were ready to sail to Lelepa Island, a steady rain began to fall. Although this day trip was a very informative and historic outing, I did not realize how dark and morbid it was. Artok Island always seemed to loom in the mist and the rain looking like a hat protecting the land from the downpour. After landing on Lelepa, we made our way to Fels Cave, where Roi Mata was taken after being poisoned. The cave was a much-welcomed respite from the rain and a place where various rock art could be found. There are patterns with dots and lines that show weather patterns to track the weather and predict the time to cultivate and harvest. Other drawings depicted birds, fish, and anthropomorphic figures.

There were also abstract motifs, like simple and complex geometric figures, such as triangles and angles. The oldest paintings are red spots and handprints that date approximately 2000 to 3000 years old and are attributed to the Lapita culture. The most recent paintings were from the eighteenth century. I was happy just to spend the day staring at the walls and visualizing the stories they told. But, like many tours, it ended too quickly, and off we scurried back into the rain and to the boats. As we made our way towards Hat Island, the rain got heavier, and the sea got rougher. Thus, the trip was canceled for safety reasons. I did not mind much. I really did not want to be trouncing on another grave or slipping in the mud in a mass cemetery. In 2006 the Roi Mata grave did not have the traffic of tourists that the UNESCO inscription as a world heritage site would bring two years later and beyond. For me, the island-shaped as a hat in the thick mist of the rain would be my only and lasting memory of the place—that would be good enough to me. I will let the ghosts grab other tourists' ankles.

Fels Cave, Lelepa Island, Vanuatu

—————

Like most of the world, the pandemic has hit the travel sector in Melanesia and the Pacific Islands in general extremely hard. Today, the United States has hit a sobering number of 600,000 deaths from coronavirus, while about 2.5 million deaths have been recorded worldwide. Although signs are pointing towards a lower level of cases of the virus due to vaccinations being distributed throughout the world, the tourism industry will take some time to get back to normalcy. At the start of the pandemic, the Melanesian countries quickly shut their borders, and those who made a living in the tourist sector struggled to make ends meet.

In February of 2021, Vanuatu's prime minister announced a safe travel bubble between Vanuatu and New Caledonia called the "Tamtam Bubble." The plan, which would also include Australia and New Zealand, was to open links with countries that had been Covid-free for thirty days or more. Also, in early 2021, Fiji desired to implement one-way quarantine-free travel with Australia and New Zealand amid the pandemic called the "Bula Bubble." The Fijian government believed that the country had proven to be a safe destination for travelers during the pandemic, with no reported cases for several months. Unfortunately, at the time, Australia and New Zealand had been battling Covid-19 outbreaks, and that it could be a while before this travel bubble was initiated.

Although the loss of tourism in the Pacific Islands has been a devastating blow to their economies, the Pacific Islands Forum Economic Ministers believe that the current crises could offer "the opportunity to assert a regional economy that supports Pacific priorities and to consider investments, policies, and partnerships required to secure the region's economic resilience and the wellbeing of its people now and into the future." When Melanesia reopens, it will not take long for travelers to return to those dark tourism places of cannibals, sorcerers, soldiers, and ghosts because they do not fade away. Even in these days of hiatus, they continue to live to tell their stories.

9

THOSE CURIOUS CARGO CULTS

Cult or cult family can contain several negative connotations to me. Whenever I hear the word, I typically, and perhaps a bit naively, think of down-trodden individuals who are desperate for attention and acceptance following a hysterical, charismatic leader who promises something glorious that the individuals could not find living in a normal society. I can recall how the world was shocked when thirty-nine members of Heaven's Gate Cult were found dead after committing mass suicide in 1997. This occurred in my home county of San Diego, and it was not until the dead members were found that I got to hear about the bizarre promise their leader made that a spaceship would whisk the followers away to salvation. Although most cults have a relatively small congregation, Heaven's gate attracted approximately 200 members who found the cults' belief appealing because of its blend of asceticism, mysticism, science fiction, and Christianity. In early 1997 the intense and glistening comet Hale-Bopp streaked across the sky, and the leader of Heaven's Gate believed that a UFO was trailing behind the comet. They felt that the Earth would be "recycled" or wiped clean, so it was time to catch this UFO and travel to the next level. The image of dead members lying on beds cloaked in purple shrouds is still haunting to this day. However, if anything, the cult's demise sure sucked the awe out of the great comet, which was actually quite a spectacular celestial occurrence, one that will not return until the year 4534.

Although cults seem to come and go, we generally do not hear about them until something drastic happens, such as a mass suicide or a battle with law enforcement. While I was doing some research, particularly on the Internet, before my first visit to Vanuatu in 2006, I kept coming across the term "Cargo Cult" that seemed to be found not only in Vanuatu but could also be seen throughout Melanesia. Cargo cult was a term used to describe groups in the late nineteenth and early twentieth century who worshipped the material wealth from the western civilizations. A stereotype often associated with cargo cults was that a leader would claim that, through a dream, a supernatural power had told them that a messiah and the ancestral spirit would soon return, bringing a huge supply of manufactured goods. Followers should expect vast shipments of modern luxuries, clothing, guns, and food. In anticipation of this shipment, cult members would build airstrips and warehouses. The arrival of these goods would usher in a new era where inequality, suffering, and death would cease.

When anthropologists became more interested in cargo cults and started studying them in more detail, the term "cargo cult" became known for the social and religious movements that arose from the stress and trauma of colonialism. Indeed, the creation of these religious groups was a way to resist colonialism and responded to indigenous groups' contradictory struggle between ancient traditions and modern capitalism. These cults often develop during a combination of crises. Often this was under conditions of social stress. The cults were Millenarian and were first seen in Melanesia in the wake of contact with more technologically advanced Western cultures. Anthropology professor and author Lamont Lindstrom described the Millenarian Movement as the "belief among indigenous people of the imminent arrival of spirits from the dead, bringing quantities of European goods for the loyal believers that would precede the coming of the millennium." The cults often blended Christian missionary teaching concerning the eventual millenarian resurrection of Christ with the Melanesian's own myths in which mythical ancestors would be transformed into powerful beings that would eventually return to life. Thus, the millennium would happen when the ancestors returned in airplanes or steamships, bringing Western goods (cargo) and initiating a reversal of the social order.

The cargo cults led to many ritualistic habits, which would seem strange to people living in a modernized society. Melanesia is full of rituals, and these cults have no problem creating formalities that epitomize modern, consumerist desires. Some cult members dress like United States soldiers and march around the island, or create mock radios out of straw, or light fires near their created airplane runways to pay homage to their chosen person of worship. Yet, some historians believe that this consumerist desire can never be truly satisfied. Westerners have endless opportunities to shop for their own cargo, yet the acquisition of goods never seems to satisfy them. Instead, it only intensifies the desire. The perpetual desire and the incessant drive to be better, have

more, and achieve dominance in human nature is the same
whether one lives in an American city or a Vanuatu village.

There are several common characteristics among the
cargo cults of Melanesia. A single charismatic chief who
consults with a prophet typically leads the cults. Although the
prophet predicts when their chosen deity will return with all
the materialistic goods, it is the chief's responsibility to
oversee the ceremonial preparations. Sometimes the chief and
the prophet do not see eye to eye, forcing them to split into
two cults. Other common attributes include having a myth-
dream that is a blend of indigenous and foreign elements and
expect help from the ancestors. Leaders, prophets, and
members of the cults maintain that the manufactured goods
of foreign cultures are created by spiritual means such as
through their deities and ancestors. The cults believe that
these goods are intended for them, and the foreigners have
unfairly gained control of these materials by mistake. Thus,
another common characteristic is the belief that spiritual
agents will eventually give the cult members the valuable
cargo and the promised manufactured goods.

The earliest cargo cult was the Tuka movement that came
into existence towards the end of the nineteenth century on
the main island of Viti Levu, Fiji. The traditional Fijian priest
named Ndugomoi, who renamed himself Navosavakandua
("He who speaks once"), inspired the Tuka Movement.
Navosavakandua proclaimed himself "the supreme judge of
all things who has power over life and death" and contended
that he had received a divine message urging a revival of traditional religious practices. Some of the startling and eye-
catching visual aspects of the Tuka movement were traditional ceremonies, prayer, merchandise distribution, and
events that resembled military parades. Navosavakandua also

bottled sanctified water, which he believed would offer eternal life. He believed that if the people brought back the ancient ways and honored their ancestors properly, it would lead to a role reversal of sorts—Europeans would serve the indigenous population.

The British Colonial Government caught wind of the movement and sent the Native Commissioner, David Wilkinson, to investigate. He learned that Navosavakandua proclaimed that the twin gods Nacirikaumoli and Nakausabaria, sons of the god Degei, would soon be revisiting the land. Wilkinson wrote, "The yalo spirits are congregating at Nakauvadra in preparation for Siganilewa, judgment or some other important event... for which there is to be four years preparation."

In late 1885 a Fijian Wesleyan teacher of Colo East Province wrote to colonial officials and told them that a body of troops, who were the followers of Navosavakandua, had come over from the adjoining province of Ra. At the same time, the Commissioner of the Colo East Province, Walter Carew, also wrote to the governor,

"Navosavakadua has stirred up a movement... based upon a very ingenious and dangerous compound- ing of Fijian mythology and belief with the teachings of the Old and New Testaments. He has given out that the return of Degei's two sons, lost at the time of the legendary Fijian deluge, is at hand when the world is to be upset and the *Lotu* (Christianity) and *Matanitu* (Government) driven out."

The colonial governor took steps to repress the movement and had Navosavakadua arrested, sentenced to six months of hard labor, and then exiled to the island of Rotuma, where he would spend the rest of his life.

Interestingly, the movement did not die out by removing

its leader, as the colonial government thought it would. Many cult priests found that the steady spread of Christianity and more colonial government presence continued to clash with their culture. The priests would stir up a revival of the movement to keep it alive. They even exalted Navosavakadu as a divine personage. They believed that they would receive communications from him. Fijians of the region told stories about the miracles and the counter-colonial activities that Navosavakadu achieved. Many of these tales invoked Bible stories, the distribution of loaves and fishes, and the revival of the dead. The colonial British were the only ones who could not punish the cult leader in these stories. Presently, the stories of Navosavakadua take place in a Fijian time and space that are both Fijian and Biblical in many dimensions.

One of the more bizarre movements among the native villages—mainly centered near missions and plantations in Papua New Guinea—was called the Vailala Madness. The madness broke out between 1917 and 1919, spreading like wildfire to the villages connected to Europeans. Once again, the movement was based on the revelations of local prophets that the ancestors were withholding European material goods from the indigenous people. As the islanders incorporated what the prophets were saying into the missionaries' sermons, they began adapting their traditional beliefs with Christian doctrines drawing some quirky conclusions. For example, upon hearing that a person goes to heaven after he dies, the natives inferred that all who die would be born again with white skin, therefore, concluding that all white people were actually reincarnated natives. The islanders eventually understood that the white men did not actually manufacture all the goods the Europeans had. Instead, they determined the white people's goods were really presents the spirits in heaven had entrusted to the whites to deliver to the natives.

In Jens Bjerre's book, *The Last Cannibal*, published in 1958, the author quoted a native who explained what happened next during the Vailala Madness:

> "They [the natives] wanted these goods, and as they couldn't see any direct way of getting them, they turned towards their traditional superstitions. By the help of magic rites they would implore their forefathers' spirits in Heaven to send the goods to them direct by ship or plane. The more they talked about it, the more they persuaded themselves that this was how it could be made to happen! They gradually worked themselves up to a frenzy of grievance, and the movement spread to other villages along the coast. Some places they laid a "welcome" table ready for the forefathers' spirits to come along with all the goods they wanted. It was a white man's table they laid; with white tablecloth, tin plates and white man's dishes."

Rumors spread that the spirits of heaven would send a large ship fully loaded with materials, including rifles and ammunition that would be used to drive the Europeans out of the country.

The madness interrupted the entire rhythm of daily life in the villages. The fields and gardens went untended because the natives believed it was unnecessary to work in them anymore since everything they needed was supposedly on the way. Some of the villages began to build large huts where islanders placed stones, sticks, and piles of leaves as symbols of guns and goods for when they arrived. On various dark nights, the natives would imagine that they saw a ship nearing the village. They would then run out of their huts, swing burning torches, and shout in a frenzy with excitement. Bjerre wrote,

> "The oddest thing was that this madness in many cases resulted in hysterical attacks of cramp. When they were seized by their delusions, their bodies would shiver, they swung their arms violently about and shook their heads madly, finally falling down and writhing in pain while the froth poured from their mouths. Some got the "gift of tongues" and shouted a lot of gibberish, which no one could understand. It was believed that the spirits were talking."

The bout of "cramps," or hysteria, became contagious to everyone throughout the village. Improvised insane dances and songs were initiated—the songs were sometimes corrupted hymns learned in the mission church.

The end of the movement came when the plantation owners along the coast expressed their concerns to local authorities under the colonial government. The Europeans really had no idea that this movement was happening until the plantation owners felt that their lives were at stake. The colonial authorities dealt with the hysteria as colonial governments typically did by suppressing and removing. They had the worst fanatics exiled, and their huts burned. Sadly, in some cases, the hysteria became their own undoing when natives in one village near Bogia District in the northwest Madang Province burned down their own huts, ruined their gardens, slaughtered their pigs, and sat for several days on the beach waiting for the ship that their ancestral spirits would bring to them. Although the madness continued here and there throughout the country in places such as the highlands for a few years, it eventually died out or was reimagined in a different form according to the caprices of the natives by 1931.

The most active period of the cargo cults in Melanesia came during and after World War Two. Two powerful adversaries, Japan and the United States poured into many isolated islands, bringing advanced weapons and supplies. The Americans, in particular, sought to occupy small, relatively unguarded, and strategic islands in the Pacific Islands so that they could eventually island-hop their way to Japan. For many of the indigenous populations of these tiny islands at the time, it was their first encounter with people from Western civilization, and it was definitely their first contact with the intimidating and fearsome machines of war. The vast amount of military equipment that the Japanese and the Americans airdropped to troops on these islands meant drastic changes to the islanders. Besides military equipment, the villagers experienced for the first time items such as canned food, manufactured clothing, medicine, tents, radios, cigarettes, and candy—to name a few. Soldiers on both sides often shared these items, or "cargo," with the natives, who believed that all these new goods were incredible and magical. Often the natives would retrieve things from misplaced airdrops or salvage the items out of the trash. Such items were seen as a source of luxury and a symbol of the wealth and power of the mysterious foreigners, deemed as divine gifts; they began to worship the deities they believed were responsible for bringing them.

When the war ended, the military went home, taking the equipment and supplies or dumping them into the sea, leaving very little with the islanders. In response to this absence of cargo, charismatic leaders developed promising access to material by catching the attention of the cargo deities. In attempts to get material to fall by parachute or delivered by planes and ships, the islanders began to perform elaborate rituals and ceremonies. Some groups imitated the same practices they had witnessed the military personnel use, copying the day-to-day activities and dress styles, making landing strips, carving headphones from wood, and fashioning large effigies of aircraft out of tree branches and leaves. On the landing strips, cult members would use signal fires and torches to light up runways. Many islanders thought that if they continued their dedicated worship and practices, the cargo would come, and their land would be turned into a paradise. However, they often felt a sense of bitterness towards foreign soldiers who they believed were in some way intercepting their shipments from the gods.

Although many cargo cults eventually gave up staring into the sea and sky, waiting for their ship or plane to come, some survived and continue to pique the interest of anthropologists and admirers of these cultural oddities. Perhaps, the most famous of all the cargo cults to survive to the present is the Jon Frum movement on the island of Tanna in Vanuatu. Jon Frum Day is celebrated on February 15th. It is a sacred day and was prophesied as the day of his return—though it is uncertain exactly which year this will happen. Frum predicted that Americans would return to Tanna, and good things would rain down upon the people. Villagers celebrate the day by painting U.S.A. upon their bodies, marching with wooden rifles, raising American flags, and building crude effigies of airplanes. The John Frum movement is by far the most studied of the cargo cults with its quirky history.

The beginning of the movement could be traced back to the arrival of missionaries on Tanna in 1841, converting many islanders to Christianity by 1900. The missionaries made a law called "Tanna Law," which created a court system presided over by Christian chiefs and special policemen whose job it was to make sure everyone (including those who still lived by *kastam*) abided by the new law. Tanna Law also prohibited kava drinking and other traditional customs. Thus, the Jon Frum movement was originally a call for traditional people to unite and fight against the threats to custom life that Tanna Law created and encouraged people to hold on to their traditional beliefs. In 1940 a custom man once told the story that Jon Frum came from Green Point (south Tanna) because he was very sorry that the customs of the islanders were disappearing, and if he had not come, Tanna would have lost all its traditional customs and practices. The custom man said, "At midnight one night, there was a meeting at Green Point. Jon Frum appeared. This appearance and his words to maintain custom encouraged people to stand strong against the missionaries. The Administration and the missionaries were worried about the events and began to imprison many islanders. But more Jon Frum followers were coming out from other parts of Tanna too."

Much has been written, and interested people ask if Jon Frum was a real person or a spirit. There are no photos of John Frum, nor have there been any relatives who have come forth to vouch for his existence. Although accounts vary, the most popular legend claims that John Frum was a stranger who arrived on Tanna around 1938, promising all kinds of unrealistic precedents—the old becoming young again and the arrival of treasures if the islanders returned to their cultural ways. Some say he was a leader who inspired his people to resist colonial oppression, while others believe he was an illusion created by unscrupulous men and used to gain power.

Yet, some accounts state that he was an American military man scouting the region before World War Two or that he was a spirit who could turn himself from a man into a tiger. Another intriguing description of Jon Frum occurred in 1941 when Presbyterian Reverend J. Bell gave a report at the Presbyterian Synod about the same incident at Green Point that the custom man shared:

"Strange happenings at a place called Green Point. Roughly twelve months ago meetings were called secretly and took place in a clearing cut out of the bush, with a huge banyan tree over all to shut out the light from the sky. They took place at night and no light was allowed, not even the glow of a cigarette or a pipe. Chiefs and elders and others were given positions befitting their rank, near to Jon Frum. A few bold spirits tried to peer into his face, but his face was well hidden by a big hat. When he spoke it was in a falsetto voice and he said little. He was said to have told the chiefs they were fools to work for the Government for nothing."

The arrival of American service members throughout Vanuatu in 1942 was not why the Jon Frum Movement began, but it did contribute to its development. When military bases in Vanuatu, especially in Luganville on the island of Espiritu Santo, began to swell with American servicemen, the presence of the soldiers had a lasting impression on the Jon Frum movement and gave the movement an American connection. Hundreds of Tannese worked alongside Black American soldiers, who looked as if they had an incredible amount of wealth that the islanders had never seen before. The Tannese saw material goods being delivered from the skies that came from the distant horizon in aircraft and on ships and witnessed military drills, marches, and men wearing military uniforms. Watching Black American soldiers of rank giving orders to white men also provided a lasting belief that their savior, Jon Frum, was about to return. As they waited for the return of Jon Frum on Tanna, runways were cleared in the jungle, and wharves were built to receive the cargo of "good things" that will help their communities just as the planes did when they dropped cargo loads to soldiers to help them win the war. Members of the cult also worshipped wooden crosses that were painted red. The common belief was that these red crosses symbolized the red cross that Black American medics wore during the war and were seen generously helping the wounded without asking anything in return.

Today, there is still a debate on the reasons why the Jon Frum movement exists. Some researchers believe that the movement represents a cultural interpretation of Christianity, where Jon Frum is a Christ or a Messiah-like figure. Other researchers think that Jon Frum was always a pagan movement but used Christian terminology to win back converted islanders. The more popular reason for the movement is that scholars see that Jon Frum is a reaction to European oppression and a precursor to Melanesian Nationalism. Perhaps, the movement is bigger than just one man; it is a cultural revolution. Maybe, Jon Frum has truly already come when independence was established in 1980. When visiting Tanna, a traveler can easily see the cultural pride on a person's face. In fact, one will notice how people proudly display their traditional beliefs throughout the entire Melanesian region. This is the reason why the Jon Frum movement keeps going—it is a way to defend the continued encroachment from Western civilizations wanting to change the traditional practices to a more capitalistic approach. Or, maybe the members of the Jon Frum movement are simply just fanatics.

One late, rainy afternoon, I was working in the Archives of the Archdiocese of Fiji in Suva. The Archives was a small, one-room area and not open to the public, so there were never any concerns about being distracted by the coming and going of patrons. A wood table barely fit in the corner of the room but allowed just enough space to do some processing and preserving work. Sometimes archives work could be pretty rote, especially when one performs the same routine on record after record on a balmy afternoon. From the window behind me, the sound of the rain over-filling gutters and falling rhythmically onto the pavement put me in a kind of Zen-like stupor. The students at the all-girls St. Anne's Primary School, which was next door, began to sing their final songs before going home for the day. A song must have been constantly in the girls' hearts because no matter where they were, either in class or on the playground, they sang all day long. Whenever I worked in these archives, I always enjoyed being serenaded by the singing students of Saint Anne's.

Nevertheless, on this afternoon, I happened to see a picture of a red cross, which pulled my attention away from my work. I stared at it; the rain got heavier, drowning out the cherub's voices from next door. For some odd reason, the picture of the red cross reminded me of the John Frum cargo cult who painted their crosses red. I can recall looking deeper at this picture wondering how a cargo cult could be considered a religion. Their faith just seemed so hopeless. Then I started to wonder if all religions started out the same. All of them, including the cargo cults, have their rituals and ceremonies. God would then bless them with good health and wealth if these rituals were done correctly. All religions share some kind of assembly attendance, even if it meant meeting at a makeshift airstrip and holding up carved wooden rifles. This will make God happy until they do it again the following week. Many churches and denominations also have a heritage that allows them to believe that what they do is right or the best way. And what is a church without liturgy? Every religion has candles, bells, glass windows, choirs, incense, chants, and effigies of aircraft- whatever they need to engage in holy behavior and worship. The picture of the red cross made me ponder a lot of questions about religion and churches. But who was I to ask whose religion was right or wrong?

A clap of thunder then exploded from above and ruptured my thoughts. The rain subsided. My colleague Katherine then burst through the door, a bit drenched and a little bit frustrated. As a teacher at one of the Catholic schools in the area, I could tell she had a hard time getting free to come to the Archdiocese headquarters to help me with the project that we were working on together. Plus, the downpour did not make it any easier to get around the city. I said, "Bula (hello)," as she sat down and plopped her purse on the floor. Katherine apologized for not getting to the archives earlier. I understood as she had a full plate every day. She picked up some documents and started cleaning them. "Come across anything interesting today?" She asked without looking in my direction. I scoffed.

The entire collection we were working on was literally bursting with fascinating historical records dating back to the 1800s. But all I could think about at the moment was the picture of the red cross. "The usual stuff today," I answered. All of a sudden, it got extremely hot in the room. Katherine then stood up and went to turn on the air conditioning. The room cooled down within minutes. I looked one last time at the picture of the red cross and wondered if the John Frum

Movement, or any cargo cult, would someday have an archive like this one. I leaned back against the window and felt a soothing breeze (more so than an air conditioner could provide) come through the window and blow upon my neck. I then closed my eyes, listening to singing girls whose song seemed to pick up where it left off during the downpour. Sometimes you just have to pause and take in the moment, especially in the heat of the afternoon. Katherine sang along, and I thought that there was nowhere else on earth I would rather be at that moment.

The Cathedral of the Archdiocese, Nicholas House, and St. Anne's School, Suva Fiji

Today, the Jon Frum Movement remains very active, and the obsession for cargo is as strong as ever. However, it has experienced some changes in its belief system that resulted in several different branches. In 2003 a branch of the movement made headlines worldwide when a breakaway leader named Prophet Fred led 300 followers and settled in Sulphur Bay, Tanna. Fred believed that this new location was closer to Yasur volcano, a spiritual site for the islanders. A land dispute ensued with rival Chief Isaac. Hundreds of men from both branches clashed using axes, bows and arrows, and slingshots. They burned down thatched huts, churches, and houses. The Vanuatu Mobile Force was asked to intervene, evicting the breakaway leader and his followers.

In 2006 writer, Paul Raffaele interviewed Chief Isaac Wan on Tanna as he prepared to celebrate John Frum Day. Raffaele would later write an article cleverly titled, "In John They Trust," for the *Smithsonian Magazine* about his experience with Chief Isaac. When Raffaele first met the chief and leader of the cult in the chief's hut, he had items ready for the impending Jon Frum Day. A table displayed a small U.S. flag on a pedestal, a carved bald eagle, and an imitation U.S. military uniform neatly folded and placed in a circle. Their conversation was fascinating. One could debate that the John Frum Movement these days represents more of a cultural interpretation of Christianity where John Frum was a Christ or Messiah-like figure:

Chief Isaac: "John Frum came to help us get back our traditional customs, our kava drinking, our dancing because the missionaries and colonial government were deliberately destroying our culture."

Raffaele: "But if John Frum, an American, is going to bring you modern goods, how does that sit with his wish that you lead a *kastom* life?"

Chief Isaac: "John is a spirit. He knows everything. He's even more powerful than Jesus."

Raffaele: "Have you ever seen him?"

Chief Isaac: "Yes, John comes very often from Yasur to advise me, or I go there to speak with John."

Raffaele: "What does he look like?"

Chief Isaac: "An American!"

Raffaele: "Then why does he live in Yasur?"

Chief Isaac: "John moves from America to Yasur and back, going down through the volcano and under the sea."

Raffaele: "John promised you much cargo more than sixty years ago, and none has come. So why do you keep faith with him? Why do you still believe in him?"

Chief Isaac: "You Christians have been waiting two thousand years for Jesus to return to earth, and you haven't given up hope."

Touché.

In 1939 the basis for one cargo movement that, at first, seemed more economic than religious formed on the island of Malekula, Vanuatu. The movement was called the Malekula Native Company (Malnatco) and was developed by Paul Tamlumlum and two non-Christians, Kaku and Ragrag Charley. The idea of the movement was to form an indigenous cooperative company that would collectively produce copra. The funds would be used for community projects such as building schools and hospitals. Under the influence of Tamlumlum, many of the islanders converted to Catholicism, and the nearby villages were persuaded to join the company, although some refused. The French Administration imprisoned Tamlumlum for forcing people to work against their will and inciting villagers to not work for Europeans. When the war came to Vanuatu, many of Malekula's islanders went to work for the soldiers. Some company members believed in the promises of riches after the war due to their close proximity to American soldiers. After the war, Paul Tamlumlum, Kaku, and

Ragrag Charley became transfixed with the American promise of material riches and a golden future. Because they grossly exploited the Malakulans in their efforts to create roads and airstrips for the anticipated arrival of American goods, they were imprisoned on several occasions. The movement eventually died out by the end of the 1950s.

The quirkiest cargo cult of all can be found on the same island of Tanna, where the Jon Frum Movement has flourished. This strange cult known as the Prince Philip Movement began in Yaohnanan village during the 1950s-1960s and is based on a legend. The tale that has been told over the years goes like this: *a volcano's spirit joined with a local woman, and the union produced a white child who married a foreign queen.* The child was sometimes believed to be the brother of Jon Frum. When the cult members saw a portrait of Prince Philip, Duke of Edinburgh, with Queen Elizabeth II in government outposts run by the British colonists, they instantly associated the prince as the son referred to in their legend. Thus, the Prince Philip Movement was born. The mixing of the outside world with the Yaohnanan tribe's traditional values keeps their culture alive. They believe that Prince Philip is a god who originated from Tanna in human form, contains the spirit of the Messiah, and is keeping their culture alive in the United Kingdom.

When the royal couple visited Vanuatu in 1974, the faith of the Prince Philip religious sect members strengthened, as they could see the Prince in person. Chief Jack Naiva and a few other villagers got an even better look at Prince Philip when they paddled a war canoe assigned to greet the royal couple. Chief Jack later told an interviewer, "I saw him standing on the deck in his white uniform, and I knew then that he was the true Messiah... It is a memory I will always have of him...

to see him in the flesh like that, even though I know that deep inside he is more than flesh and bones."

When the Duke of Edinburgh became aware of a cult dedicated to him, he sent a portrait of himself to the village. The villagers responded by sending the Prince a pig-slaughtering club called a *nal-nal*, which the Prince reciprocated by sending them another photo of him holding the club. A shrine was erected, which included all the photos of the Prince, a Union Jack flag displayed on a bamboo pole, and was protected by Chief Jack until he died in 2009. In 2007 several cult members were flown to England to be part of the Channel 4 reality television series, *Meet the Natives*. During an off-screen meeting with the Duke of Edinburgh, the cult members presented gifts to the duke and asked him when he would return to Tanna. He ambiguously answered, "When it turns warm, I will send a message."

In April 2021, Prince Philip Duke of Edinburgh sadly passed away peacefully in his bed. He was ninety-nine years old. As the world mourned, it was only a matter of time till anyone saw how his death would affect the members of the Prince Philip Movement. Perhaps, they had been preparing for this day. Reports coming from Tanna made it look as if they were ready for this moment. Cult members conducted a ceremonial dance, held a procession, displayed Prince Philip memorabilia, and the men drank kava. Eventually, all these ceremonies culminated into a momentous and symbolic gathering as a final act of mourning. This may also be when a successor to Prince Philip is appointed—most likely will be the duke's son, Prince Charles. Until then, the cult believes that when Prince Philip's mortal form dies, his spirit will return to his spiritual home of Tanna and bring the wealth of the British crown back with him.

Many anthropologists, historians, and travelers have debated the appropriateness of the term "cargo." Some believe that it does not refer to an identifiable factual reality. The emphasis on "cargo" says more about Western ideological bias than about the movements' concerns and desires. Others have argued that the focus on cargo cult isolates the phenomenon from the social and cultural side that gives it meaning. The movements give people an intriguing look into the psychology of religion and the evolution of faith. Lindstrom examined "cargoism" more deeply and was concerned with the Western fascination with the phenomenon in both academic and popular writing. He wrote, "The name cargo cult is deeply problematic because of its pejorative connotation of backwardness since it imputes a goal (cargo) obtained through the wrong means (cult); the actual goal is not so much obtaining material goods as creating and renewing social relationships under threat." Nevertheless, cult members have had a fleeting peek into the Western world and have coveted the material to the point that they have created profound spiritual movements that have changed their lives. Until then, they continue to watch the sky for planes and the sea for ships, perhaps, in the vain hope that their cargo will one day come.

10

YOU FRIGHTEN. YOU ASTONISH.

A few years before the new Vanuatu National Library and Archives building was built, I volunteered with Anne and Augustine in the National Archives. At the time, the two were working out of a small room, the size of a broom closet, in the Cultural Center. Although the Archive room was on the first floor near the Center's loading dock, it felt like it was in the basement. A poster on the wall about the importance of sand drawing always caught my eye. Sand drawing is one of Vanuatu's unique cultural practices: part art, part storytelling, and part communication. These drawings have a deep cultural meaning, which goes beyond a rational description of the patterns they describe. They fascinate me on a creative and practical level.

In 2008, Vanuatu sand drawing was inscribed on the UNESCO's List of the Intangible Cultural Heritage of Humanity. This form of writing was proclaimed an indigenous artistic expression that occurred in a range of ritual, contemplative and communicative contexts. When visitors come to the Cultural Center museum, they are treated to an exhibition of this unique form of communication. For me, however, the poster was a nice distraction. Whenever I needed a break, it allowed me to sit and absorb the sand drawing examples that functioned as mnemonic devices to record oral information, histories, and stories. I used to think, *how does one even archive a record drawn in the sand?* It would be a very ephemeral record that could easily disappear with even the slightest gust of wind. One cannot just throw it in an acid-free folder and place it in a record carton box. Preserving the drawing would be a nightmare for any archivist.

One day after lunch, Anne, who always had pep in her step, vigorously entered the office and broke my undying and undivided poster-induced daydream. She wanted to show me the inside of the twenty-foot container housing records to be processed for the National Archives. The entire Cultural Center was strewn with boxes of records—in the attic, the stairwell, underneath tables in the library, and along the walls and aisles of the building—pretty much any space where a box could be placed was used for storage. I snapped out of my coma and went outside to the container only a few feet from the loading dock. As we were looking at the contents of the container, which looked like a cyclone went through it spewing paper and boxes all over the place, a group of museum workers and *kastom* men were moving and preparing artifacts for shipment. The men were participating in the 2010 Melanesian Art and Culture Festival in New Caledonia. Anne and I could not help but try to get a closer look at the unique art pieces that were meant to make their way to the festival. Although I noticed that a couple of the men gave me a disparaging glance, I knew better than to touch anything. About an hour later, a woman from the Cultural Center came to the Archive office and reprimanded Anne for being too close to the artifacts. It was *kastom* taboo for a woman to be near the artifacts. In typical Melanesian form, the men would not say anything to us at the moment and instead went a long way around asking another employee of the Center to come and talk to us. It was an odd moment, and Anne was a bit flummoxed for innocently disrespecting *kastom* space. However, I tried to take the blame, stating that my curiosity made me encroach too close to the artifacts, dragging Anne with me.

Making these innocuous cultural *faux pas* at the most random time is what made Melanesia utterly fascinating. These are countries with unwritten customs and rules. There are secrets, a lot of secrets that go unobserved by the aloof and insensitive tourist. But, when one lives and works among the Melanesians, the fabric of the culture becomes very slowly unraveled piece by piece. Even Anne once told me that after living in Vanuatu for over forty years, she still does not comprehend the complexities of *kastom*. Superstitions are widely believed, rarely discussed, and will force behavior that enforces taboos. It is dark on these bright, idyllic islands, as taboo is bound by some kind of supernatural threat that is usually termed "danger" and certified by some specific conse-quence, most commonly, infection by some powerful mystical force. This might have dreadful society-wide consequences, cause psychological or physical sickness, or some reversal of personal fortune to a person and their loved ones. Because Anne was a woman who got too close to the artifacts, the *kastom* men truly believed that something horrendous would happen and rightfully acted according to their customs. The men were not rude. They were just averting a potentially harmful situation that they perceived because of their super-stition.

The zenith of written stories about the region took place in the early half of the twentieth century. With its picturesque, unspoiled atolls, beautiful, loosely dressed native women, and its cultural clashes with Europeans and Western perceptions, Polynesia seemed to attract many writers. Herman Melville, Mark Twain, and Robert Louis Stevenson were a few of the first writers to arrive in Polynesia who wrote about their experiences. Although the missionaries were the ones who recorded some of the earliest Melanesian cultural superstitions and taboos, it was the fiction writers that captured the essence of the region and used many of the dark cultural practices in their themes and backdrops.

Between 1900 and 1950, many writers such as Jack London, Robert Dean Frisbie, James Norman Hall, Charles Nordhoff, and Somerset Maugham ventured to the South Seas and became captivated by its pristine innocence. All the writers were disgusted by how the colonists and missionaries were stripping culture away from the islanders. This flagrant rape of traditions became the theme behind a multitude of stories. Many of the authors who came to Polynesia returned home while a few stayed and lived out the rest of their life on a serene, palmy island. But regardless, the indelible impression that the people, custom practices, and environment of the Pacific Islands had on these writers would stay with them throughout their writing careers.

The dark islands of Melanesia did not attract as many writers to its unpredictable, white sandy shores surrounded by a dense jungle interior. Nevertheless, a few authors were attracted to the foreboding and sinister islands rife with rumors of cannibalism, headhunting, and sorcery.

Beatrice Grimshaw, mentioned numerous times throughout this narrative, was one of the first fiction authors and the first woman writer who used Melanesia as a backdrop for her stories. Grimshaw's books shed extensive light on the political and social scene of the Melanesian Islands at an important moment in history. The combination of text and photography in her books highlighted her experience. She represented an early-twentieth-century woman, independent and mobile, intrigued by the prospect of adventure, missionary work, and scientific exploration. Many of Grimshaw's characters were missionaries, displaced indentured indigenous laborers, ostracized European professionals, beachcombers, and outcasts, entwined in the complex realities that played out on multiple levels of the social and racial hierarchy among the islanders and Westerners.

I like to think of Grimshaw as the first female romance writer who captured the Victorian Age and the white woman's experience in the colonized Pacific. Like most writers who came before and after her, she wrote about the islanders, but she did not necessarily write for them. To the contemporary audience, her writing might seem a little offensive—she, perhaps, blindly believed that the Melanesians were not only dying out but welcomed their suppression by a "fitter" race. Her writings were socially and politically very conservative and at times insensitive. She would praise a traditional dance or ceremony and belittle an indigenous worship place by stealing an idol.

Like the other authors who stayed and wrote about the Pacific, Grimshaw, too, found it important to not "turn native." She despised the white settlers who she thought had fallen from grace and rebelled against the colonial hierarchy. She distanced herself from the Westerner who became a beachcomber, a "remittance" and the "ne'er-do-well" man.

The writers noticed that when a white man "turned native," he lost a certain respect from the natives. Grimshaw wrote:

"Honesty, sobriety, and industry repay their possessor as almost nowhere in the world. Yet, with all this, the white settler in the Pacific Islands is generally of a more or less undesirable kind...There are men who have 'gone native' in most of the Pacific groups, living in the palm-leaf huts with the villagers—but a white man in a waistcloth and a bush of long hair, sleeping on a mat and living on wild fruit and scraps given by the generous natives, drunk half the time and infinitely lower, in his soberest hours, than the colored folk who unwisely put up with him, is not a happy spectacle."

At the height of her career, Grimshaw was very well-liked and known to a broad audience. As a woman, she never felt that she was distinguished or memorable. But as a woman traveling and living alone in Melanesia, she was an anomaly in the early twentieth century to the Europeans and islanders that she encountered. She captured this in her writings.

Grimshaw would retire to Bathurst, New South Wales, Australia, in 1936. She would continue to correspond with a young man in Papua New Guinea, enabling her to maintain her reputation for depicting accurate backdrops in her adventurous romance novels; she died in 1953. Although her books are now out of print, they can still be found in various publishing outreaches on the Internet.

Another prominent fiction author who contributed to bringing Melanesia to a broader audience of readers was Louis Becke. George Lewis (Louis) Becke, who at a young age changed his name to Louis Becke, was born in Port Macquarie, New South Wales, Australia, in 1855. At the age of sixteen, he stowed away on the ship *Rotumah* that was bound for Samoa.

His real-life saga was more exciting than any fiction he would later write for American and British readers.

He would work on the ship *Leonora* as a supercargo for three months, captained by a notorious and disreputable buccaneer of the Pacific named William Henry (Bully) Hayes. A supercargo on a Pacific ship was an important post during the nineteenth and early twentieth centuries. These men kept accounts and operated a trade room—a kind of seagoing country store. Traders on various islands had to be supplied with different types of material to trade for the islanders' copra, palm oil, or any other native product. Becke would invite island chiefs to the trade room and swap brandy, rifles, clothing, and other amenities for coconuts, turtle shells, and copra.

In March 1874, the *Leonora* was boxed in between a couple of whaling ships while at anchor in the Utwe Harbor at Kosrae during a cyclone. Becke survived the shipwreck and was also able to save a considerable amount of stores, weapons, and ammunition from the ship. Soon afterward, Becke quarreled with Hayes because of the way Hayes treated the islanders, which sometimes led to bloodshed. Hayes argued that Becke was part of a conspiracy to lower his prestige and lessen his authority with the other white men and the islanders. Thus, the two parted ways, and Becke went to live in the village of Leasse. He would remain in this village for the rest of his stay on the island. Twenty-five years later, Becke fondly recalled the villagers who accepted him in Leasse, "I can never forget the kindness, warmhearted hospitality, and amiability that filled their simple hearts to overflowing." Becke eventually left Korsae when the British warship *H.M.S. Rosario* arrived in hasty pursuit to arrest Hayes and his crew for piracy. Hayes evaded arrest on a technicality, but Becke was taken to Brisbane for trial. However, for lack of evidence, he was acquitted from all charges of piracy.

Becke would try to live a more simple life in Queensland, Australia, for the next few years. Although he did participate in the Palmer River gold rush, most of his jobs were actually quite mundane for someone of his ilk. He worked at the Ravenswood Station in 1877 and became a bank clerk in Townsville the following year. But the call to seek new adventures throughout the South Seas was too strong. In 1880 he took a job for a firm from Liverpool, England, on the island of Nanumanga in the Ellice Group (Tuvalu today), where he ran a trading station. He then opened his own trading store on Nukufetau, where he married an island woman named Nelea Tikena. Later that year, wanderlust would get the better of him, and he boarded the ship *Orwell* leaving his island wife behind. It was unclear exactly where he was going. However, the shipwrecked in the Beru atoll, Kiribati and Becke lost most of his possessions. Fortunately, the ship *George Noble* called on the island, and Becke made his way to Sydney.

Between 1881 and 1882, Becke took a dangerous post at a trading station in New Britain, New Guinea—his first foray into Melanesia. He was on constant guard against cannibals and malarial fevers that would not only cut his time short on the island but would disable him for the rest of his life. From New Britain, he learned about a colossal French colonizing deception perpetrated by the French nobleman Charles Marie Bonaventure de Breil, Marquis de Rays. The Marquis de Rays called the colony La Nouvelle France. There were at least three different expeditions to La Nouvelle France between the years of 1870 to 1882. To attract people to the territory, he marketed it as an existing, well-established, and thriving colony through advertisements, word of mouth, and a journal of the

de Rays' own publishing company, *Nouvelle France*. In his journal, he brought to public attention his plans of converting and
then colonizing the Pacific Islands and exclaimed that there
was a bustling settlement and the land flourished with fertile
soil. But, this truly did not exist. Although the French government rejected his ideas, enough people believed in his fore-
sight and signed up for an expedition.

In 1880 the third expedition, known as the de Rays Expedition, became the most infamous. Four ships named *Chan-
dernagore, Gentil, India,* and *Nouvelle Bretagne* set sail to Port
Breton, New Ireland, carrying about 570 unprepared colonists
from France, Germany, and Italy. The entire venture would be
disastrous. For example, the 240 Italian colonists, who made
the journey aboard the *India* to escape their poor living conditions in Italy, were required to pay the Marquis 1,800 francs
each in gold or could offer their services in labor for five years.
In return, the emigrants were promised twenty acres of land, a
four-bedroom house, a thriving settlement, and supplies.
Sadly, none of this would happen. For three months, the
Italian colonists lived in appalling and cramped conditions
aboard the ship. Diseases easily spread, and food was in short
supply. When they did reach Port Breton, there was no busy
settlement or rich grazing lands. Supplies never arrived, and
many died mainly from malaria.

The ill-fated expedition would result in 123 deaths from
starvation and sickness, and the survivors would eventually
go to Australia or New Caledonia. In 1882 the Marquis de Ray,
who never visited the colony, would be arrested for fraud and
sentenced to six years in prison, and he would die in a French
asylum in 1893. Louis Becke would eventually write a story
entitled "The Awful Duel on Utuan," which portrayed the
aftermath of the Nouvelle France colony fiasco.

Although Becke's South Seas wandering lifestyle was full of illness, shipwrecks, and bad luck, he continued to seek new adventures and collect knowledge about islanders' languages and customs. It was not until 1892, when he returned to Sydney, that his life roving about the Pacific came to an end. Unable to find work, Becke wrote his adventures, adding even more flair to the stories. A year later, the editor of the *Sydney Bulletin*, J.F. Archibald, suggested to Becke that he could package the stories and send them to his friend W.H. Massingham, the editor of the *London Daily Chronicle*. After reading the stories, Massingham enthusiastically wrote Archibald about the stories, "I think them extremely strong—incomparably stronger than Stevenson's work, which seems to me clearly derived from them." Being compared and equaled to Stevenson was unheard of in those days (and at any time) and was very high praise. In 1957 James Michener would respond to a question to identify those who really knew the Pacific and was the best writer about the Pacific. Without hesitations, he said, "If you want an honest, evocative unpretentious and at times fearfully moving account of the Pacific in its heyday, you must read Louis Becke."

As an author, Becke traveled and lived in various places worldwide, including the United States, Canada, England, Ireland, and Jamaica. He would meet other significant literary figures such as Rudyard Kipling and Mark Twain. Sadly, Louis Becke would die alone in a Sydney hotel room in1913 from recurrent bouts of malaria, rheumatism, and throat cancer. He was found sitting in a chair with a manuscript of an unfinished story scattered at his feet.

Louis Becke would publish approximately thirty-five books, six collaborating with Walter James Jeffrey and proving popular with readers. His first book, By Reef and Palm, would go through seven London printings in ten years. He wrote about the islanders and their interaction with Europeans, traders, and missionaries. He sometimes took a pessimistic view of the "civilizing" influences of the Western settlers and adventurers who came to the Pacific. Although many of his characters lived a free life away from society's conventions, they often indulged in crime, adultery, and cruelty. In several stories, Becke's main character was Tom Denison, a South Seas supercargo—actually Becke's alter ego. A reader could tell that this cheerful, carefree lad would dive into the author's autobiography. By contrast, he would use the infamous and nefarious Bully Hayes, the seafaring captain of the notorious blackbirding ship, *Leonora*. He controlled with a "steel fist and a pair of pistols," as the villain, or reprobate in several stories.

Bully Hayes was the type of pirate that inspired many South Seas writers who wanted to develop a rapscallion in his story. He was born in 1827 in Cleveland Heights, Ohio, and bounced around the United States working with the U.S. Revenue Service, a captain on a Great Lakes steamer, and even joined the U.S. Navy, allegedly serving under the revered Admiral David Farragut. In the mid-1850s, Hayes landed in Honolulu, Hawaii, and was remembered as a man who was "over six feet in height, big, bearded, and blond, with a soft voice and a persuasive smile—240 pounds of intriguing manner and sly scheming."

Hayes's first recorded arrival in Australia was in Fremantle in 1857 as the master of a ship that he acquired by devious means in Singapore. In 1859 the San Francisco Bulletin also described Hayes by informing its reader, "The brig, *Ellenita*, Captain Hayes, ran off on Sunday night without clearing papers and leaving creditors to the amount of several thousand dollars in the lurch. The captain pretended that he was about to sail to Melbourne and obtained credit for the repair of the vessel and large amounts of stores, besides the baggage of intending passengers, with all of which he put off on an unknown and unlawful voyage."

Over the next couple of decades, Hayes would travel the Pacific Ocean between California, Hawaii, Australia, New Zealand, and the Caroline Islands. In the mid-1860s, he got involved with the Maori War in New Zealand and made quite a bit of money smuggling powder and ammunition to the natives at hidden coastal anchorages. The intrepid sea captain could have gone on for years as an unscrupulous trader, engaging in bold maritime frauds and acquiring women he picked up at various islands and dropped off whenever he tired of them. However, he decided to venture into the notorious and lucrative blackbird business. The mention of the name "Bully Hayes" caused many islanders, especially Melanesians, to hide in fear of being kidnapped and shipped to be a laborer on some distant plantation. It was also reported that he would team with another notorious blackbirder named Ben Pease and terrorize the islanders throughout the Pacific. Hayes's end came as violently as his life was lived.

Although there are many versions of his death, it most likely occurred on the ship *Lotus* in 1877 while cruising in the Marshall Islands. After a quarrel with a sailor, purportedly the ship's cook, the sailor stabbed Hayes with an iron fitting and cast his body overboard. Despite being a scoundrel, Hayes was also remembered for being a fascinating companion who could sing the songs from German classical composers in a fine voice, was an accomplished performer on the piano and violin, and spoke several languages, including various Polynesian dialects. It is no wonder that the man attracted the attention of many South Seas writers.

James Michener was, perhaps, the last great writer from the west whose stories focused on Melanesia as a backdrop. His 1947 Pulitzer Prize-winning novel, *Tales of the South Pacific*, and his follow-up work *Return to Paradise*, published in 1951, were actually a grouping of tales that added up to a short story collection. Though *Tales of the South Pacific* showed an unusual structure and narrative voice that confounded critics and reviewers, Michener defended his work by stating, "This is not a standard novel and could not be handled in a standard way. What worked for him was a loose collection of delicately interrelated stories in which no one character, setting, and concept assumed priority. War is sloppy. Men move in and out of relationships. And in the end, things drift apart." Author Stephen May, who wrote a biography about James Michener, believed that Michener's *Tales of the South Pacific* was essentially an existential novel. "It is about fragmentation, unresolved conflicts, momentary gain, and lives left dangling. Trying to deal with intolerable reality or a diverse group of military personnel struggling with the moment. War always lurks like a dark, unseen force beyond the island." One of Michener's strengths in his Pulitzer Prize-winning novel was his ability to capture the speech patterns of the Melanesians. It also probed the friction between American and Pacific cultures. *Tales of the South Pacific* was Michener's first novel, and *Return to Paradise* was his third book. It was he who brought Melanesia to the American audience, and it was that mystical and magical island of Bali Ha'i that still clings to the American consciousness to this day. Michener would always feel a special fondness towards the South Pacific throughout his life. He would write over forty novels during his career;

still, his story backdrops and characters never returned to Melanesia.

Since Michener, there has not really been a Western fiction author who has come to prominence or has produced the output with Melanesian themes as those of the famous South Seas writers from the first half of the twentieth century. Plenty of nonfiction narratives have been written and, perhaps, dominate the current interest in Melanesian lore. Nonfiction authors such as missionaries, anthropologists, military service members, historians, and inquisitive adventurers have informatively and profoundly contributed to the history and culture of this unique part of the world from the last half of the twentieth century to the present day. Be that as it may, it begs the question—what about the status of Melanesian writers?

A few fiction and nonfiction writers from the region have sprung forward in the last few decades, and their works are worth mentioning. For example, New Caledonia can boast a couple of authors who are part of a dynamic literary scene. Pierre Gope is a Kanak writer whose works include poetry and plays. Déwé Gorodey is another Kanak politician and writer who evokes the struggle for independence in her writing and gives a feminist view of Kanak culture. Vincent Eri was considered the first Papua New Guinean to write a novel in English, *The Crocodile*, published in 1970. Vincent's countryman, Julie Mota, has become a well-respected writer, poet, and artist. The Solomon Islands can boast of being the home to two terrific writers, Jully Makini and Rexford Orotaloa. As a poet and writer, Makini writes about women's rights in the Solomon Islands, where violence against women is still an issue that is taboo and difficult to discuss within society. Orotaloa is best known for writing the novel *Two Times Resur-*

rection. Like Makini, Grace Molisa is a Ni-Vanuatu poet and politician who also fought for women's rights. *The Australian* newspaper had described her as "A vanguard for Melanesian culture and a voice of the Vanuatuans, especially women." Arguably, the most renowned artist from Vanuatu is Marcel Melthérorong, an author, poet, storyteller, playwright, producer, musician, and songwriter. Born in Nouméa, New Caledonia, but now calling Vanuatu home, Melthérorong projects express collective creativity, sharing, and harmony.

The author, Epeli Hou'ofa, was the consummate Pacific writer whose work resonated in the Islands. Born in Papua New Guinea to Tongan missionary parents, he lived and taught in Fiji and eventually became a Fijian citizen. Hou'ofa passed away in 2009, but his body of work spanned a diversity of genres; poetry, novels, nonfiction, and satirical short stories. In his writings, he responded to the imperialist view of all of Oceania as scattered, isolated entities in need of external guidance. To him, the ocean became a space of connection and intimacy. Like the other Melanesian writers, Hou'ofa did not write to expose the customary dark secrets of Melanesian, but rather, he was more concerned with the conflict between modern and traditional culture and the way Melanesia existed in a changing environment dominated by Western ideas, technology, and opinion.

During my last couple of visits to Vanuatu between 2012 and 2014, I invariably spent my free time hanging out in the Gallery Blong Vanuatu shop located up the hill on the Kumul Highway and just outside the capital town of Port Vila. The shopkeeper's name was Renol, whom I called Reynold for a couple of years. He was a talented musician with a big smile and a soft voice. Most of the time, I could not understand a word he would say to me and vice versa, and thus, we got along splendidly. I do not believe he was a Francophone who spoke only French (along with Bislama and his village language), but he just spoke English in a soft mumble. His store was a little bit off the beaten tourist track and was never bustling with shoppers. A couple of tables were set up so that he could serve assorted beverages and snacks. Although I came to the shop for the friendly companionship, I stayed for the sausage rolls and the Wi-Fi, which was undoubtedly better than the motel where I was staying. Plus, he did not charge me for Internet use. After work at the Vanuatu National Archives, I would make the short walk to the shop, and Renol would always greet me with a smile and a bottle of water and say something to me that I did not understand. Sometimes he would pull out a traditional instrument like a flute or a drum and start performing as if I was the first person to enter the store that day which I believe was often the case. We would then have a conversation about two completely different subjects, and I would whip out my laptop to catch up on the day's emails and other Internet things.

On many occasions, Renol would disappear for a while from the shop to have a smoke and a chat with any passerby that he knew or with the employees from the Toyota car store next door. When this happened, I would sometimes take a break from what I was working on and aimlessly browse the shop's authentic collection of wooden artifacts, masks, and carvings. As I examined the collection of traditional items, it was evident that the Melanesians artistically excelled. Along the far wall was an impressive row of ornately carved *tam-tams* (slit drums) ranging from three feet to approximately ten feet tall and having various decorative faces. When looking more deeply into the faces of the drums, I could feel some kind of magic or enchantment exuding from the carved wood.

There were times when I thought, *man, this would look great on my front porch, but what kind of juju does it contain?* Indeed, every artifact in the store had a story behind it, and Renol never shied away from passionately telling it, although, I admit, I usually had a hard time following along. As I stared at a ten-foot drum one day, Renol elbowed me and said, "You take home." I chuckled. At the time, I could barely afford the sausage roll. "You take home," he repeated.

"Reynold, I'll never be able to get it through customs." I could just see myself trying to lug that log through LAX's customs. I foresaw a customs officer giving me that, "are you kidding me?" stare.

"I ship to you." Renol enthusiastically added. He constantly thought that I was from Australia as Aussies were predominantly the employees, volunteers, and tourists who came to Vanuatu. Regardless, the drum weighed more than a hundred pounds, and the shipping cost would have been astronomical and way more than the cost of the drum itself. I smirked, shook my head, and apologetically declined, though it would have been awesome to have something like it in my home. It definitely would have been a conversation piece, and I would have been the coolest kid on the block, especially after I beat it a few times. On my last visit to the shop, Renol gave me a two-foot *tam-tam* for free. "You take home. Gift. Show family and friends. Tell everyone about Renol." I graciously accepted, and on the flight home, I remembered thinking, *maybe someday I will get a chance to talk about Reynold.*

For centuries Melanesia has been composed of oral societies. Writing down stories did not begin until after the colonial governments had packed up and left. However, Melanesians have been practicing a unique and diverse form of artistic expression through artifacts composed of woodcarvings, sculptures, paintings, masks, and statues. When the islanders created these artifacts, they did so without any intent that these items would be "art." Instead, the artifacts were conceived as an integral part of everyday life's religious and social ceremony and were also used as forms of ancestor and spirit worship. Although fertility, ancestor figures, and the human head were common themes among art, other sinister motifs described such practices as headhunting and cannibalism. As one could imagine, the artwork created in this part of the world had a more ominous appearance, perhaps, because Melanesian philosophy perceived a world where the dead and living, natural and supernatural, coexisted in close association. Often, the living had to defend themselves against the jealousy of the dead. This resulted in constructing ghastly, garish designs for magical precautions against the ghosts. Thus, images of the dead were mingled with totemic animals such as crocodiles, lizards, and sea birds that were used to decorate and bless many of the everyday objects like assembly houses, canoes, drums, and masks for dancers.

The creation and practice of Melanesian artistic artifacts would experience a decline throughout much of the twentieth century. Colonialism and the influx of missionaries contributed to the disruption of artistic traditions among indigenous groups. Many islanders often neglected, discarded, and even actively destroyed art forms. Many times they incorporated songs, dances, and masks into Christian rituals. In the 1920s and 1930s, numerous scientific expeditions and a multitude of individual anthropologists, adventurers, and explorers encroached upon the region and documented the indigenous arts and culture. A bounty of Melanesian artifacts were sent to museums and universities in Australia, Europe, and the United States. In fact, surrealist artists of Europe were influenced by the haunting wood-carving sculptures placed on display. The French writer and poet André Breton, a leader in the surrealist movement, was fascinated and admired the sculptures from the Western Pacific. To Breton, Melanesian art looked liked a counter-argument to the orderly bourgeois civilization that he and other surrealists came to disdain. He observed that the sculpted Melanesian figures had grossly elongated or shortened limbs, and their faces were distorted by exaltation or anguish. The figures "seemed complete and formally perfect and yet, also in the process of transformation into some new identity." In a poem about Uli, a series of statues of an ancestor figure carved by the Mandak people of central New Ireland, Papua New Guinea, Breton wrote, "You frighten. You astonish."

From the late twentieth century to the present day, there has been a revival in the creation of traditional arts throughout Melanesia. Traditional visual and performing arts previously neglected are now being rejuvenated and rediscovered by new generations of Melanesians. This art revival is also being spurred on tourism. For example, the Arts Council of Fiji, a government-funded agency, encourages village artisans to practice their traditional skills and sell their works to visitors through handicrafts fairs held throughout Fiji during the year. A series of contemporary art movements have also emerged, pioneered by artists such as Mathias Kauage of Papua New Guinea. In Nouméa, New Caledonia, the Tjibaou Cultural Center was built in 1998 and was the first major institution to primarily showcase works by contemporary indigenous artists from the Pacific. The Melanesian Arts and Cultural Festival was conceived by the Melanesian Spearhead Group and currently takes place every four years. The goal of the festival is to promote traditional and contemporary arts from all of Melanesia. The first festival took place in the Solomon Islands in 1998. In 2014, the festival welcomed Melanesian communities from the Papuan provinces of Indonesia, Timor Leste, and the Torres Strait Islanders of Australia into the festival.

A tam-tam (slit drum), Vanuatu

The same kind of traveler attracted to dark tourism is also attracted to collecting dark artistic artifacts. Although obtaining a sorcerer's pouch or a cannibal fork can feel like a macabre experience, Melanesian-made masks and slit drums draw the most attention and have become very popular among tourists. Because every aspect of life in Melanesia became strongly influenced by religion and ritual, masks are one of the main ritual objects used to represent the features of the deceased. They were also made to protect the deceased by frightening away evil spirits. Additionally, besides honoring the dead, masks established a relationship with the spirit world. Sometimes, they were used to force the spirit of the newly dead to depart for the spirit world.

Melanesian slit drums, on the other hand, refer to large hollow tree trunks with a slender slit and can be played in an upright position or lying on the ground. The drums can be decorated with elaborate sculptures that indicate their strong relationship to the ancestral world. The drums are played in ceremonies with the function of calling the ancestor spirits. They can also send out acoustic signals and messages to the population or even to call individual persons. They played an important role in earlier times by calling the appropriate men for a headhunt, signaling their return, and performing the following rituals with the captured heads. Among certain villages in Papua New Guinea, the slit drum—or as it is known in Tok Pisin, *garamut*—are considered to be living social agents that encourage relationships in the political, social, and religious realm. Although the *garamut* could be used in private and village ceremonies and informational transmission, it is also used for spirit communication. Villagers believe that certain spirits called *ggnumtik* live in the forest and are credited with giving voice to the *garamut*, especially from the part of the slit in which the voice or sound is produced. The spirits are either considered members of the village or are only known to some people or individuals. Thus,

certain *garamut* can be possessed or have personal characteristics of a spirit whose presence is acknowledged to be present
in the slit drum.

Row of tam-tams, *Vanuatu Cultural Centre*

While one of the best ways to experience the Melanesian
culture is through art, whether attending a festival, a kava
ceremony, or visiting a *kastom* village, I have found that it is
only a glimpse into their mysterious way of life. Their traditions are like a dormant volcano that runs deep, is dark and
profound, and at times explodes with modern Western values.
To Melanesians, the environment is the source of their physical, spiritual, and intellectual nourishment. It has defined and
confined them to an area where a tremendous diversity of
cultural and linguistic features developed over time. The
Melanesian system of social, economic, and political organi-

zations, beliefs, values, cultural norms, and practices was designed to establish balance, satisfy every villager, and maintain social order. Even today, there are communities throughout the region that depend on their traditions to survive.

Melanesians see themselves living in complete harmony with the animal, plant, and spirit world. They do not think of themselves as masters of the universe. Rather, they believe that they are just an essential component in an interdependent world of the person, the animal, the plant, and the spiritual. Although they are diverse in many cultural practices, they are united by a common vision that has evolved over thousands of years. Bernard Narokobi, a lawyer, international consultant, author, lecturer, and philosopher from Papua New Guinea, once wrote, "I see a new vision and a new hope for Melanesians. I see ourselves holding fast to the worthy customs of our people. I see Melanesians accepting principles of Christianity. I see Melanesians giving their highest regard to the spirituality of human dignity and a proper but insignificant role to the building up of status through materialism." Narokobi believed that the Melanesian voice should be conceived as a positive, creative, and constructive force aimed at the good, the beautiful, and the just.

Today, Melanesians have come to the crossroads of living in the reality of their ancestral customs and lands, as well as a modern State where the spread of Western culture, economic practices, and individualism has threatened their cultural identity. For decades the Melanesians have only known themselves through books written by others, but now is the time to show the world the uniqueness of their civilization, philosophy, and culture. When I travel around the region, it is easy to feel that these are countries that developed a dependency on foreign governments or donor aids—a detriment for communities to solve problems for themselves. But when I look closer, I can see that the "Melanesian Way," or voice, is more at the heart of their culture. An integral part of this voice is characterized by how they value land and community rather than possessions and the *wantok* system of building relationships through exchanging gifts. Despite their history of headhunting, cannibalism, and sorcery, the most essential part of Melanesian society is its close human relations. Villages may be overlooked as third world, but when examined more closely, one sees a vital and dynamic institution that is a cultural unit and an instrument of civilization, technology, agriculture, and enterprise. Cooperation and mutual support is another critical value among villagers, especially during times of crisis. This was evident, for example, in Vanuatu in 2015 when Cyclone Pam pummeled the archipelago, especially on the island of Tanna. Although the islanders experienced massive devastation, they showed exceptional courage and resilience in the storm's aftermath. Cyclones are a part of life in Vanuatu. Each member of the community knows how to support one another during the response and recovery stage and come together to share food, resources, replant crops, helping those who are most affected.

Throughout Melanesian, there was a maxim that has been around for ages, and even Narokobi mentioned in his writings about how the people of the region had found the meaning of life: "Live well, love well, have something good for every person, and die a happy death." Narokobi despised how personal human relationships were sacrificed for professional titles and how tragic it was that political parties further divided the Melanesians.

Happy Solomon Islands children

In this age of the Covid-19 Pandemic, his statement could not have been further from the truth. A little more than a year after the start of the pandemic, the virus has killed more than two million people worldwide, and in the U.S. alone, it has incredibly taken the lives of over 550,000 people. But, the virus has done even more damage as it has exposed deep political, economic, and racial cuts and scrapes that seem very unlikely to heal anytime soon. Fortunately, the advent of vaccines has provided more optimism throughout the U.S. and the world. But even with the vaccinations, the number of cases is still on the rise in certain states, and the vaccine distribution has also become politically polarized. However, states are now rushing to reopen despite distressed appeals from health experts to move more cautiously.

When I drive on the freeway, I see a large sign painted on the side of a storage unit that reads, "We Are in This Together." However, the sign never truly registers with me. There is still this distrust, anger, and frustration among the people that bubbles to the surface each time a new development occurs. Even the Black Lives Matter movement remains in an early stage of reform and now could include Asian Americans as they have been recently targeted and violently attacked. An inevitable cultural revolution feels imminent in the air, but when, how long, and at what cost? I can only close my eyes and think, *live well, love well, have something good for every person, and die a happy death.*

The U.S. is not in this alone; the virus is a global problem, and no country is safe until every country is safe. Although vaccines have arrived in Melanesia, the entire Pacific Islands have been even more isolated with the closure of their borders. Although the past year has not been easy for many islanders, especially those who thrive on tourism, they remain optimistic despite the uncertainty about how long this crisis will last. Even as the number of people who receive vaccinations increases, they know not to let down their guard. Islanders realize that it takes a collective effort to fight Covid-19 and protect their families, friends, and communities. Their sense of community responsibility is their most significant asset and provides strength to reestablish and believe in the secret of life. *Live well, Love well, have something good for every person, and die a happy death.* They are, indeed, in this together.

By the time I return to Melanesia, over two years will have passed since my last visit. It is a part of the world where time can easily stand still, and I oddly take comfort in this fact. Even in these almost unbearably and hot and humid islands, life could 'freeze like a raindrop on a sub-zero day' with or without a pandemic. But this is okay. I have ultimately learned that volunteer projects will wait. My nonprofit mission will wait. Colleagues will wait. *Kastom* will wait. The ghosts of the past will wait. The dark secrets that lurk in the jungle will wait. The pesky insects that carry away my snacks in the middle of the night will wait. The waiting just simply blends together where a day has never passed.

Moreover, during this dormant time, I watch, wonder (always wondering), and write. Melanesia is a mystifying, magical place full of worldly and unworldly people guided by a common cultural and spiritual unity. Although it is intriguing to examine the dark side of culture in these once labeled "dark islands," it is yet, a place of bright inspiration full of centuries of unique wisdom and enlightenment. Those cherished moments of the smell of the frangipani flower, the crackling of beach coral under my feet, the sweat dripping, the taste of the muddy water of kava, the refreshing dip in a blue lagoon, the feel of torrential rain falling on my head, and the infectious smiles of the islanders, will forever remind me to *live well, love well, have something good for every person, and die a happy death.*

ACKNOWLEDGMENTS

My favorite part of completing a new project is to graciously thank all those who have made it possible for me to get to that last period. I would first like to give my sincerest gratitude to the many colleagues throughout the Pacific region, particularly in Melanesia, who helped me create a home away from home over the past several years. I would like to give the most sincere recognition to my Melanesian colleagues turned friends, Opeta Alefaio, Kabini Fa'ari, Katherine Foi, Abilyn Pua'ara, Bernard Rizu, and Augustine Tevimule. They shared their culture and helped make this project possible. Special thanks to Anne Naupa, Bishop Terry Brown, and Catherine Green, whose experience working and living in Melanesia provided valuable insight into the many and unusual facets of traditional expression. You guys are the true adventurers.

I am also immensely grateful to publisher Frank Eastland of Publish Authority. Frank's enthusiasm and curiosity towards a project where the subject matter takes place in an enigmatic part of the world inspired me to tell more. I am immensely grateful to my editors, Nancy and Bob Laning, whose comments, suggestions, and inquisitive interest in the Melanesian culture led me to an infinitely stronger manuscript. A special thanks goes to Raeghan Rebstock for devoting her time and talents helping to create a wonderful cover for the book. And cheers to the whole team at Publish Authority for making me feel like I am the only writer out there.

Finally, I would be remiss not to acknowledge those who have been instrumental in supporting me when I was nose-deep into the writing process. To Patricia Black for her eagle eye proofreading, and now can proudly admit that she knows where Melanesia is. My deepest gratitude goes to my wife, Shannon, whose understanding of my absence throughout the day and night to work on the project is, as always, well appreciated. We can now return to that backlist of horror movies to watch together. Another hearty thanks goes to my daughter and biggest fan, Devin—sorry that this is not like a Sarah Mass novel; I assure you that Melanesia can be full of fantasy as well. Lastly, I would like to recognize my cat, Alice, who never missed an opportunity to sprawl upon my research and kept me company throughout the entire project.

ABOUT THE AUTHOR

Brandon Oswald studied archives and records management at the University of Dundee, Scotland. He is the Founder/Executive Director of the nonprofit organization Island Culture Archival Support (ICAS) that is dedicated to providing voluntary archival assistance to cultural heritage organizations in the Pacific Islands. Brandon has had several papers about cultural preservation in the Pacific Islands accepted at major international archival conferences. He is the author of the book *Mr. Moonlight of the South Seas: The Extraordinary Life of Robert Dean Frisbie*. Brandon lives in San Diego County, California, with his wife, daughter, and three cats

SELECTED BIBLIOGRAPHY

BOOKS

Bjerre, Jens. *The Last Cannibals*. Pan Books, 1958.

Day, A. Grove, editor. *Louis Becke South Sea Supercargo*. The Jacaranda Press, 1967.

Department of Education Papua New Guinea. *A History of Papua New Guinea and its Neighbors*. The Jacaranda Press, 1990.

Dixon, R.M.W. *"We Used to Eat People" Revelations of a Fiji Islands Traditional Village*. McFarland & Company, Inc., 2018.

Edwards, Philip editor. *James Cook: The Journals*. Penguin Books, 2003.

Fischer, Steven Roger. *A History of the Pacific Islands*. Palgrave, 2002.

Forsyth, Miranda. *A Bird That Flies with Wings: Kastom and state justice systems in Vanuatu*. ANU Press, 2009.

Grimshaw, Beatrice. *From Fiji to the Cannibal Islands*. London, Eveleigh Nash, 1907.

Grimshaw, Beatrice. *Isles of Adventure*. London, Herbert Jenkins Limited, 1930.

Kanairara, Philip and Derek Futaiasi. "The Belief in Sorcery in Solomon Islands." *Talking it Through: Responses to Sorcery and Witchcraft Beliefs and Practices in Melanesia*, edited by Miranda Forsyth and Richard Eves, ANU Press, 2015, pp. 281-296.

Kent, Graeme. *Company of Heaven: Early Missionaries in the South Seas*. Thomas Nelson Inc., 1972.

Knox, Margaret. *Voyage of Faith: The Story of the First 100 Years of Catholic Missionaries Endeavour in Fiji and Rotuma*. Archdiocese of Fiji, 1997.

Kwai, Anna Annie. *Solomon Islanders in World War II: An Indigenous Perspective*. Australian National University Press, 2017.

Lightner, Sara, and Anna Naupa. *Histri Blong Yumi Long Vanuatu*. Vanuatu Cultural Centre, 2005.

May, Stephen J. Michener's *South Pacific*. University Press of Florida, 2011.

MacClancy, Jeremy. *To Kill a Bird with Two Stones: A Short History of Vanuatu*. Vanuatu Cultural Centre, 2002.

McCotter, Clare. *Colonising Landscapes and Mapping Bodies: Imaging Tourist Space & Place in Beatrice Grimshaw's Travel Writing*. 2005. University of Ulster, PhD Dissertation.

Michener, James A., and A. Grove Day. *Rascals in Paradise: True Tales of High Adventure in the South Seas*. Random House, 1957.

Montgomery, Charles. *The Shark God: Encounters with Ghosts and Ancestors in the South Pacific*. HarperCollins Publishers, 2004.

Moorehead, Alan. *The Fatal Impact: An Account of the Inva-*

sion of the South Pacific, 1767-1840. Harper & Row Publishers, 1966.

Mythinger, Caroline. *Headhunting in the Solomon Islands: Around the Coral Sea*. The MacMillan Company, 1942.

Nanau, Gordan Leua. "Wantoks and Kastom (Solomon Islands and Melanesia)."

The Global Encyclopedia of Informality, Vol. 2, edited by Alena Ledeneva, UCL Press, 2018.

Narokobi, Bernard. *The Melanesian Way*. Institute of Papua New Guinea Studies and the Institute of Pacific Studies, 1980.

Randall, Will. *Solomon Time: An Unlikely Quest in the South Pacific*. Scribner, 2002.

Stokes, Donald S., collector, and retold by Barbara Ker Wilson. *The Turtle and the Island: Folk Tales from Papua New Guinea*. Hodder and Stoughton, 1978.

Taylor, John and Nick Thieberger, editors. *Working Together in Vanuatu: Research Histories, Collaborations, Projects, and Reflections*. Australian National University E Press, 2011.

Thomas, Nicholas. *Cook: The Extraordinary Voyages of Captain James Cook*. Walker & Company, 2003.

Williamson, Rick. *Cavorting with Cannibals An Exploration of Vanuatu*. The Narrative Press, 2004.

JOURNALS

Aime, Alphonse. "Unwrapping the social and cultural meaning of Garamut (slit-drums) of Papua New Guinea." *Contemporary PNG Studies DWU Research Journal*, vol. 25, November 2016, pp. 54-66.

Ammann, Raymond. "Middle Sepik music and musical instruments in the context of Melanesia." *Journal de la Société des Océanistes*, 146, 2018, pp. 179-188.

Bradshaw, Ann Lane. "Joseph Conrad and Louis Becke." *English Studies,* vol. 86 no. 3, 2007, pp. 206-225.

Brantlinger, Patrick. "Missionaries and Cannibals in Nineteenth-Century Fiji." *History and Anthropology,* vol. 17 no. 1, 2006, pp. 21-38.

Gardner, Susan. "A "vert to Australianism": Beatrice Grimshaw and the Bicentenary." *Hecate,* vol. 13 no. 2, 1987, pp. 31-50.

Idusulia, Penuel. "The Beliefs About Spirit Powers in the Area of North Malaita,

Solomon Islands." *Melanesian Journal of Theology,* vol. 18 no. 2, 2002, pp. 122-127.

Kaplan, Martha. "Meaning, Agency and Colonial History: Navosavakadua and the "Tuka" Movement in Fiji." *American Ethnologist,* vol. 17 no. 1, February 1990, pp. 3-22.

Kolshus, Thorgeir and Even Hovdhaugen. "Reassessing the death of Bishop John

Coleridge Patteson." *The Journal of Pacific History,* vol. 45 no. 3, 2010, pp. 331-355.

Laracy, Eugénie and Hugh Laracy. "Beatrice Grimshaw: Pride and prejudice in Papua." *The Journal of Pacific History,* vol. 12 no. 3, 1977, pp.154-175.

McCotter, Clare. "Seduction and Resistance, Baptism and 'Glassy Metaphorics":

Beatrice Grimshaw's Journeys on Papua's Great Rivers." *Hecate,* vol. 32 no. 1, 2006, pp. 81-99.

Mombi, George. "The Death of Christ and Its Meaning for Melanesians from Paul's Letter to the Galatians: From Fear to Freedom." *Melanesian Journal of Theology,* vol. 29 no. 2, 2013, pp. 79-162.

Nongkas, Catherine and Alfred Tivinarlik. "Melanesian

Indigenous Knowledge and Spirituality." *Contemporary PNG Studies: DWU Research Journal*, vol. 1, 2004, pp. 57-68.

Roth, G. K. "Model Spirit Houses from Fiji." *The Journal of the Polynesian Society*, vol. 62 no. 4, 1953, pp. 406-409.

Waldroup, Heather. "Picturing Pleasure: Fanny Stevenson and Beatrice Grimshaw in the Pacific Islands." *Women's History Review*, vol. 18 no. 1, 2009, pp. 1-22.

ELECTRONIC RESOURCES

Photograph of Beatrice Grimshaw (from Frontispiece of *From Fiji to the Cannibal Islands*) Grimshaw Origins and History website, http://grimshaworigin.org/prominent-grimshaw%20individuals/beatrice-grimshaw-south-pacific/. Express permission granted by Thomas W. Grimshaw. Accessed 16 February 2022.

"Cargo Cult." *The Spiritual Life*, 23 February 2021, https://slife.org/cargo-cult/. Accessed 18 March 2021.

"Dark Tourism sites: should we be visiting them?" *Intrepid Travel Journal*, 2 June, 2016, https://www.intrepidtravel.com/adventures/dark-tourism-sites/. Accessed 4 February 2021.

"Remembering Roi Mata, the Last Great Chief of Vanuatu." *Bula Kava House*, 14 May 2014, https://blog.bulakavahouse.com/2014/05/14/remembering-roi-mata-last-great-chief-vanuatu/. Accessed 5 February 2021.

Bourscaren, Durrie. "In Papua New Guinea's Sorcery Wars, A Peacemaker Takes on Her Toughest Case." *npr*, 24 May 2018, https://blog.bulakavahouse.com/2014/05/14/remembering-roi-mata-last-great-chief-vanuatu/. Accessed 16 July 2018.

DeCarlo, Tessa. "A Gibson Girl in New Guinea." *Smithsonian Magazine*, April 2016, https://www.smithsonianmag.

com/travel/a-gibson-girl-in-new-guinea-114490653/.
Accessed 24 September 2018.

Dennis, William G. "Dumbos, Black Cats, and Cosast-watchers during World War II." *Warfare History Network,* https://warfarehistorynetwork.com/2019/12/20/dumbos-black-cats-and-coastwatchers/. Accessed 8 April 2020.

Eves, Richard and Angela Kelly-Hanku. "Witch-Hunts in Papua New Guinea's Eastern Highlands Province: A Fieldwork Report." *Australian National University,* 2014, https://www.researchgate.net/publication/265168928_Witch-Hunts_in_Papua_New_Guinea%27s_Eastern_Highlands_Province_A_Fieldwork_Report. Accessed 4 August 2018.

Forsyth, Miranda. "New Draft National Action Plan to Address Sorcery Accusation-Related Violence in Papua New Guinea." Australian National University, 2014, http://dpa.bellschool.anu.edu.au/experts-publications/publications/1246/new-draft-national-action-plan-address-sorcery-accusation. Accessed 4 August 2018.

Forsyth, Miranda. "Responses to and issues arising from recent cases of sorcery Accusation related violence in PNG." *RegNet Research Papers,* 2016, No. 122, https://papers.ssrn.com/sol3/papers.cfm?abstract_id=2869615. Accessed 5 August 2019.

Gopal, Avinesh. "The Sacred Value of Cannibalism in Fiji." *Pacific Islands Report,* 25 February 2014, http://www.pireport.org/articles/2014/02/25/sacred-value-cannibalism-fiji. Accessed 24 September 2018.

Hamilton, Scott. "Surrealism Blong Vanuatu?" *EyeContact,* 12 May 2017, https://eyecontactmagazine.com/2017/05/surrealism-blong-vanuatu. Accessed 7 April 2021.

Hayward-Jones, Jenny. "Melanesia New Voices: Investing

in the Next Generation." *Lowy Institute*, 26 June 2015, https://www.lowyinstitute.org/publications/melanesianew-voices-investing-next-generation. Accessed 20 March 2021.

Koone, Rich. "African Americans in World War II, the Asiatic-Pacific Theater." *Texas Historical Commission*, 5 February 2014, https://www.thc.texas.gov/blog/african-americans-world-war-ii-asiatic-pacific-theater. Accessed 4 August 2020.

Raffaele, Paul. "Sleeping with Cannibals." *Smithsonian Magazine*, September 2006, https://www.smithsonianmag.com/travel/sleeping-with-cannibals-128958913/. Accessed 24 September 2018.

Smith, Amy. "Melanesian cargo cults and the unquenchable thirst of consumerism." *Goodnews*, 17 July 2018, https://www.newhistorian.com/2018/07/17/melanesian-cargo-cults-consumerism/. Accessed 17 March 2021.

Trueman, C. N. "The Battle of Guadalcanal." *History Learning Site*, 19 May 2015, https://www.historylearningsite.co.uk/world-war-two/the-pacific-war-1941-to-1945/the-battle-of-guadalcanal/. Accessed 8 March 2018.

Usborne, Simon. "Dark tourism: When tragedy meets tourism." *National Geographic*, 5 November 2020, https://www.nationalgeographic.co.uk/travel/2018/02/dark-tourism-when-tragedy-meets-tourism. Accessed 4 February 2021.

Wong, Tessa. "Prince Philip: The Vanuatu tribes mourning the death of their 'god'." *BBC News*, 12 April 2021, https://www.bbc.com/news/world-asia-56713953. Accessed 12 April 2021.

Young, Peter T. "Bully Hayes." *Images of Old Hawaii*, http://imagesofoldhawaii.com/bully-hayes/. Accessed 26 September 2018.

THANK YOU FOR READING

If you enjoyed *The Darklands: A Melanesian Experience*, we invite you to share your thoughts and reactions online and with friends and family.

Publish Authority

www.ingramcontent.com/pod-product-compliance
Lightning Source LLC
Chambersburg PA
CBHW070102030426
42335CB00016B/1977